When Soul Appears

AL MCGEE

 FriesenPress

One Printers Way
Altona, MB R0G 0B0
Canada

www.friesenpress.com

Copyright © 2022 by Al McGee
First Edition — 2022

All rights reserved.

No part of this publication may be reproduced in any form, or by any means, electronic or mechanical, including photocopying, recording, or any information browsing, storage, or retrieval system, without permission in writing from FriesenPress.

ISBN
978-1-03-912118-8 (Hardcover)
978-1-03-912117-1 (Paperback)
978-1-03-912119-5 (eBook)

1. RELIGION, SPIRITUALITY

Distributed to the trade by The Ingram Book Company

Introduction

IN SHORT, THE soul is not a fixed entity. According to Father Sylvan, it is a movement that begins whenever man experiences the psychological pain of contradiction. It is an actual energy, but one that is only at some beginning stage of its development and action. Every day, every more or less average human individual experiences the appearance of this energy in its most embryonic stage. Whenever there is pain or contradiction, this energy of the soul is released or "activated." But almost always, almost without any exceptions whatsoever, this new energy is immediately dispersed and comes to nothing. A hundred, a thousand times a day, perhaps, "the soul is aborted." An individual is completely unaware of this loss and remains so throughout his whole life.[1]

It went from cold, disapproving looks and scolding until the day when the man of the cloth (the senior pastor) lost control and shouted me down. (I was his associate in a large church.) Why the outburst? I think it was related to colossal personality differences and very different ways of being in the world.

I don't think the Rector ever quite knew what to make of me, his opposite, a contemplative who aspired to prayerful time and space for introversion and reflection. A bull in a china shop, the Rector was a frenetic personality—always hurrying and scurrying about. He wished to remake me as a business manager like himself and I was a preacher/teacher. I dug in my heels, fighting for my life. We were a bad fit from the start, and it got worse and worse as the months dragged on. I used to feel under his cold, censoring eyes that I couldn't do anything right, and after a while dreaded going to work.

The senior pastor could not relate to my sort of personality whose first book purchases at Seminary were *New Seeds Contemplation* by Thomas Merton, *Mysticism* by Evelyn Underhill, and *How to Meditate* by Lawrence LeShan.

I absolutely loved the writings of British author Colin Wilson, who wrote almost two hundred books on inspired levels of consciousness. Wilson's writings are filled with his immense positivity: "When I open my eyes in the mornings, I am not confronted by the world, but by a million possible worlds."[2]

I discovered Wilson's book *The Outsider* early in my career. Wilson wrote: "Ask the outsider what he ultimately wants, and he will admit that he doesn't know. [Why?] Because he wants it instinctively, and it is not always possible to tell what your instincts are driving towards. That is, the outsider is in the grip of an intensity of a passion that he may not understand but cannot help but follow. He is driven to a creative way of being that others may not care about or understand at all."[3]

Alas, the Rector had hired just such an outsider and surely had more than he could cope with. He didn't understand me, and I didn't comprehend that my pronounced differences could drive another man to the brink.

The former senior pastor of the church intervened and urged me to get out fast. He warned me that things would never change, and an explosion was coming. Indeed, my failure to manoeuvre my way out, and my continuing presence, brought on the tsunami.

On that fateful day when I got blasted, I was utterly dazed. It was soon afterwards that something died inside of me. It was the death of my dream to be a church pastor. I knew that the dream no longer had any traction. I knew that I could not, or perhaps rather would not, go on.

When Soul Appears

Up to that time, I had conceived of no other possibility than to be a Protestant minister. I had been a minister—the Reverend Al McGee—for more than ten years. That was my identity, and it had been hard won.

Now reeling from the angry verbal assault, I was left with a sense of shock and disbelief. I really couldn't believe what had happened. How could it have come to this? It was quite a state to be in, but strangely, I also felt a sense of relief and, mysteriously, a sense of triumph.

How could that be? I should have perhaps felt suicidal. Instead, I began to feel liberated. I felt a surge of strength and a resolve that I would never allow myself to be treated that way again.

This meant that I wouldn't try again to be a pastor. "Why would you go on, anyway?" a dear friend exclaimed. "You have no respect for any of the clergy. You're not one of them." She was right, but it took the verbal lashing to break my attachment.

Later, as I was driving along a highway, a thought nearly knocked me out: *I do not believe*. I repeated it loudly several times. I surprised myself to be thinking the unthinkable and saying the unsayable: "I do not believe." But instead of censoring myself, I said it louder: "I do not believe. I do not believe!" I was shouting at the top of my lungs, renouncing everything.

"Where did that come from?" I asked, stunned. I didn't know that was in me! And who was saying it? Surely not the one known as the Reverend Al McGee. I didn't recognize that protesting self. He had never appeared before. I had always believed—even during rebellious teenage years, I had believed. I had raised hell a few times, but I had always believed. Now I was proclaiming: "I do not believe. I do not believe," and was amazed to be surging with joy and elation.

The effect of the defiant protest seemed to be making room, or clearing space, for something else to appear. It was an inner movement of cataclysmic proportions, an explosion from within my own psychic depths. By feeling free enough to say that I did not believe, some inner power was being unleashed. Thus empowered, I felt free enough to question everything, and I didn't feel judged or condemned.

A spiritual revolution was going on inside of me as I drove along that highway. It was the sense of moving into another dimension of myself—a part of me that had been somewhat hidden and buried. Another life was now surging forth, like a dam unleashed, without the slightest fear of disapproval or censorship.

And here's the insight, as I put words to paper: I was entering another life. A sense of soul was exploding inside of me. Soul was appearing in a dramatic way. I would never again care about becoming established and recognized as a minister or pastor. Something higher and deeper was breaking through. Everything else seemed false and artificial in contrast.

From then on, my life was all about whether that newly appearing sense of self was appearing in all its fullness and power. I was beginning then, I now realize, to live from within. To live, in a word, authentically. I could not live in any other way.

My experience, as painful as it had been, was something good. There was something in it that was the upside of down. Some hitherto unrealized, coiled-up potential had become unstrung.

It was exhilarating and transforming. I was brimful with life and inspiration. Where was this feeling going to lead? Well, life is full of surprises!

A while later, I attended a yoga class for the first time. The teacher, probably the most experienced yoga teacher in Calgary, wanted to say something to me almost as soon as she met me. I was startled at the way she spoke to me. Her warm presence and searching eyes were a palpable force. I felt recognized, valued, and understood on the spot. She recognized something in me that the angry clergyman had tried his best to cast out. I felt she was drawing out some hidden, buried part of me that had longed for expression but had been suppressed in other contexts.

Within minutes of meeting me, Margot Kitchen, the Director of the Yoga Centre of Calgary, exclaimed, "There's a video, Al, that you must watch. I'll get it for you."

When I got home, I put the video on and watched as Bo Lozoff, whose ministry was to teach prisoners how to meditate in their cells, gave a talk at the Mount Royal College in Calgary, Alberta. Bo was sitting, not standing, at the front of a lecture hall. He was sitting cross-legged, which I'd never seen before.

Bo had no title.

No pulpit.

No Bible.

No priestly attire.

But more amazing and astonishing to observe was just how natural and casual he was. Bo wasn't performing. He was simply being Bo, and you could have heard a pin drop when he began to speak. As I watched Bo, I began to weep. For Bo was Al. In Bo, I was seeing my future.

Over the next few years, I would find my voice and style more than ever before as I created the Calgary Yoga Academy. There I would sit cross-legged at the front of the room several times a day. I was no longer the Reverend Al McGee with a title, Bible, or pulpit. I was just being Al. And I would deliver my homilies. People used to say that the Academy was better than any church they'd ever been to.

Al McGee

I had been teaching yoga for ten years or so when a student appeared who stood out from the others. I used to feel she was watching me with her glowing, penetrating eyes. And then one day, she handed me a piece of paper. "Al, this is a poem about you." It's called '*Man of God.*'

> No collar wears he
>
> Man of God.
>
> No golden cross for all to see
>
> Man of God.
>
> No flowing robes or sermon book
>
> Man of God.
>
> But he hath breathed the holy flame
>
> And drunk the blood of the lamb
>
> Man of God.
>
> And he hath wept in green pastures
>
> And layeth down by still waters
>
> To softly whisper your name
>
> Man of God.

I was astonished to read the poem—astonished by the grace of it.

When Soul Appears

During those years at the Calgary Yoga Academy, I used to deliver homilies in every class.

Like these:

Chapter One:
When Soul Appears

WHEN, IN THE Star Wars episode, *Return of the Jedi,* the mask of the dark Lord, Darth Vader, comes off, an exceedingly vulnerable man is revealed—a frail, dying man. Formerly impenetrable, the unimaginable is now revealed. He is an open man, a real one, and now no longer a menacing figure. No longer invincible, and no longer terrifying. In his weakness, no longer in power or control, we catch a glimpse of the soul of a man who had looked like he had no soul. For a moment, as he lies dying, the soul of Darth Vader appears.

It's been a startling image for me—this image of a broken man whose soul finally appears—ever since Joseph Campbell first drew attention to it in the series of interviews on PBS called *The Power of Myth*. A thought has been with me ever since: human beings can be most real in just such a state of total brokenness.

A state of brokenness can be the means whereby the soul appears. When all has been stripped away, what remains is something true and real about you. And then:

Connection is possible.

Friendship is possible.

Understanding is possible.

And healing is possible—as in this instance with the formerly sinister Darth Vader and his son, Luke Skywalker.

What we see is that when Darth Vader's soul appears, there is an immediate sense of contact and communion with Luke. My take on this is that a key to communion and understanding is a kind of shattering of the mind, as Joseph Campbell, the literature professor and renowned mythologist, explained. The mind must not be in control, for it can only really be itself in relation to the heart. When the mind is out of sync with the heart, it creates friction, enmity, and broken relationships. Put simply, the mind must be humbled in order to find its own true power and depth as it relaxes into the heart.

Jacob Needleman, Professor Emeritus of Philosophy at San Francisco State University, calls the exclusive focus upon the mind an attachment to "one's eager, explaining mind."[4] A mind like this tends characteristically to "race ahead into complications and ingenuity without end."[5]

On display is a racing mind that, like a flood, sweeps aside everything in its path, meaning that when the mind is thus charging ahead, it doesn't pause to listen. Instead, its restlessness speeds up, and volume and intensity increase. Arrogantly, it races ahead, bound by a sense of its own superior certainties. It's a mind moving so fast that it skips impatiently past any kind of shared, spacious quest for truth and understanding.

An aggressive ego is on display, according to Needleman, an ego concerned to sound "clever, brilliant, or imaginative."[6] It's a mode that Needleman knew well as a young philosophy professor when he often "pushed hard to be right, original, bold, or up-to-date." Over time, he came to realize that he was bound by his own mind, and he grew weary of the effort to hone the ability to score intellectual points. He was tired, in other words, of allowing the power of his mind to block the power of soul.

When Soul Appears

Like Jordan Peterson, the University of Toronto Professor of Psychology who had a similar breakthrough, described in *Maps of Meaning*. "Something odd was happening to my ability to converse. I had always enjoyed engaging in arguments, regardless of topic. I regarded them as a sort of game. [But then] suddenly, however, I couldn't talk—more accurately, I couldn't stand listening to myself talk."[7]

A deeper force was emerging from Jordan Peterson's own psychic depths. Soul was appearing in the life of Professor Peterson. A profound inner confrontation stopped his racing, argumentative mind. The effect of the inner self-interrogation was that he began to listen: "I really had to listen to what I was saying … I spoke less often … I would frequently stop, midway through a sentence, feel embarrassed, and reformulate my thoughts."[8]

Now the danger of failing to engage yourself in this way is, according to Jacob Needleman, that you could remain stuck in a restless, hardened mind for the rest of your life. As Needleman writes: "I saw in many of my valued friends and teachers a heartless brilliance and cleverness."[9]

The alternative to being a brainiac is to learn to inhabit the whole of your being, which is regarded as an attainment in yoga. Yoga calls it "samadhi," an integrated state of wholeness in which all your parts are working well together. This is when all your parts are fully harmonized and cooperating with each other.

It's not a case of mind against feeling or feeling against mind. It's not one compartment against another. Samadhi is that state in which neither the mind nor feeling reigns, but rather all your inner faculties are aiding each other. It's a state of total self-connectedness.

The key to the attainment of the state of samadhi is the awakening of a certain inner capacity. That essential faculty is the harmonizing agent that I am calling "soul." When soul appears, it is a movement within, what Needleman calls a "vibration of one's inner being."[10]

"I clearly remember," says Needleman in *What is God?*, "the moment something deep inside me started breathing for the first time."[11] He was a young boy when, while sitting with his father, he gazed up into the sky to behold millions of stars. Awestruck, it was then that "an entirely new instrument of seeing had all at once been switched on. In an instant, a powerful neutral current of energy streaked down both sides of my spine—so quickly I had not a moment to have a thought about it or an emotional reaction to it."[12] A certain inner capacity had been set on fire. Soul was appearing in the life of Jacob Needleman.

Soul appears when we are awestruck or in a state of crisis or may emerge as the result of a state of profound self-questioning.

Another instance of the soul's appearance for Needleman occurred when he met the Zen Buddhist monk, D.T. Suzuki.

The encounter reads thus:

> I heard movement behind the closed doors. I tried to pull myself together. A nice-looking Japanese woman opened the door and said that Dr. Suzuki would see me now. The next thing I remember is not the size or shape of the room, nor the furnishings, nor the lighting, nor the kind of chair I sat in. I remember only the face and figure of Suzuki himself—especially the eyebrows, which seemed to grow out from his forehead like enormous wings. He was old, slightly built like most Japanese. I vaguely remember a cardigan sweater and a bow tie. But what I do remember very clearly was his presence. In Suzuki's presence, my mind went blank. The sight of him instantly went through my armor. For a

few moments, I was simply a naked mind neither anxious nor confident.[13]

Needleman had received a taste of samadhi, of that exquisite fullness of being that is a profound integration of mind, body, and soul. Without words, Suzuki's presence had pierced through Needleman's armour to give him a glimpse of this possible unified and harmonized state of being.

Soul may appear because of a state of extreme vulnerability, as in Darth Vader's case. Or it may appear because of great wonder, as when the young Jacob Needleman looked up to contemplate millions of stars. It may appear as the result of intense self-interrogation, as in Jordan Peterson's case. It may appear because of the disarming presence of a holy man, as in Needleman's young adult encounter with D. T. Suzuki.

Whatever the trigger, there is a sense of a deeper you, a deeper self, a more authentic self-appearing. What's false about you recedes into the background as your higher, truer, essential self appears. It's a homecoming. There's a sense of completeness and wholeness. In its fullest expression, you can feel that your greatest dreams have been realized.

An incomparable experience.

Chapter Two:
Follow the Upward Shift

A FRIEND OF mine wrote a beautiful chant, and I was there when it was recorded. For days afterwards, I woke up every morning with the chant flowing through me. I felt myself riding on a wave of grace. I was being carried by grace, and I didn't plan to get off that train of awareness at the next stop, or the one after that. If possible, I was going to remain in that delectable state of awareness for as long as possible. It was like riding on a magic carpet with a luscious sense of lightness and limitlessness.

I wasn't going to levitate any time soon, but who knows? I never left the ground, but I experienced a sense of energy rising, like a gushing fountain pulsating from my own psychic depths. I wouldn't trade a high like that for any other, for I can't imagine anything comparable.

The great yogis recommend that we take note of when this energy rises within us, however slight, and then follow it. Their word is to follow the upward shift and not stupidly get in its way. To follow the upward shift means that you are "attending consciously to this inner pulse." This requires determination: "Taking firm hold of That, the pulsating Shakti—dynamic energy—the awakened yogi remains firm with the resolution, 'I will surely carry out whatever it will tell me.'"[14]

Al McGee

I'd felt this upward shift before when I'd been chanting the Guru Gita, an ancient East Indian chant, for a two-week period. I had set apart the time each day to prepare myself for what the future might hold. On one afternoon, I finished the chant and googled "B.C. teaching jobs" with no idea that there was actually a website with that name: "British Columbia Teaching Jobs." There I discovered a posting from a private school in Vancouver, a school I'd never heard of, that was looking for an English Literature Department Head. *They're looking for my wife*, I thought.

My wife had been teaching high school English, Philosophy, and Comparative Religion for fifteen years at a Calgary private school and wasn't looking for a change ... at least not consciously!

Two hours later, when she got home from school, I quietly handed her the job description. She said nothing, but I'll never forget the look of steely resolve. She applied straightaway.

Several weeks later, we were in Vancouver for the third and final interview. We stayed somewhere where she was in one room, and I in another. In the wee hours of the morning, I thought I'd check on her. I walked gently over to the spot where I thought she'd be sleeping.

Well, she wasn't. She was sitting up. I stood there without saying anything.

Then out of the dark came these words: "Al, I didn't think it was possible to be this happy."

Rabindranath Tagore, the first East Indian to win the Nobel Prize for Literature in 1913, was an unhappy young student when a line from a poem startled him into awareness. Everything changed for Tagore when "suddenly I came to the words: "It rains, the leaves tremble."[15] Within himself, Tagore felt the action of the rain and the trembling response of the leaves. The rain was God's grace, the trembling leaves, the opening of his heart. It was a coming together in his inmost being: "At once I came to a world wherein, I recovered my full meaning. In that moment, I was no longer a mere student with his mind muffled by spelling lessons, enclosed by a classroom."[16]

For Tagore, it took a poem to create the upward shift. For me, it's been the effect of chanting.

Neither poetry nor chanting get much press these days. As Gurumayi, the Siddha Yoga Meditation Master, wrote:

> Many people shun reading holy books and chanting ancient hymns because they think it is old-fashioned. They think religious activity is obsolete and irrelevant in the modern world. They regard religion as a refuge for people with problems, people looking for easy answers, people with time on their hands. So, they look askance at spiritual practice; it doesn't fit into their schedule, they say. It is not backed up by the latest scientific discoveries. It's something toothless old folks do. It doesn't look good in the neighborhood. It doesn't fit in with modern civilization.[17]

Well, I'm not toothless … at least not yet. And chanting and poetry continue to create that exquisite upward shift into soulfulness that I am determined to follow.

Chapter Three:
Elegantly Balanced

I CAN PICTURE her even now, some twenty-five years later, a very charming woman in her early seventies trying without success while sitting in a yoga class to cross one leg over the other. My student couldn't stop laughing as she repeatedly tried and failed to get one leg over the other, which endeared her to me. I hoped she'd return to class to try again! Alas, she did not, and I haven't seen her since. I have, however, often thought of her with great affection.

Did it really matter whether she ever got one leg over the other? In one sense, no, for the deepest meaning of yoga is the freedom to laugh while making the heroic effort. Seen in this way, she was a great success at yoga. Many times, in contrast I've seen great flexibility but without grace and laughter.

I'll choose laughter and joy every time over some grim determination to succeed, but if she had come back to class, I'm sure I could have helped her to sit in an elegant and poised way. And in so doing, my student and friend would have received an important physical benefit for her hips and back. But more than that, she would have found a way of elevating her spirit even higher than it was.

This kind of posture is a bliss pose. Anyone who learns to sit in this way will find that her mind will calm and her spirit soar. This is also true if you do the same movement standing. Try it if you will.

Try standing while balancing on one leg.

Then gradually begin to cross one knee over the other.

Relax into it.

Stay there a while and then ease out of it.

Pause and notice the effects.

One thing you may notice is that your troubles have vanished. That's because by focusing this way, you effectively shut down that part of yourself that's addicted to worry and stress. By concentrating like this, you rise above your anxieties into another zone, or a higher level of being. As such, you become something of a dashing figure.

You have begun to dance like Shiva, the Lord of the dance in East Indian spirituality. And your life will improve. When you look at a picture of the dancing Shiva, the Nataraja, you'll see that the dancer is crossing one knee over the other, just as I have described. It's an elegant balancing act.

Two things are happening at once. An elevation is going on while simultaneously the life is being crushed out of a malevolent little dwarf. That dwarf is symbolic of obstacles and delusions. In other words, the dancer is rising above obstacles and barriers as he attains his own expressive, elegant, balancing act. It might even be said that this posture is an act of defiance.

The dancer is defying gravity.

He is defying limitation.

When Soul Appears

The movement involves the determination to affirm the best impulses of your own higher nature and a refusal to be a slave to the lower impulses of your baser nature.

A parallel to this can be found in the Sioux dance, where it is understood that the best dancer is the one who can keep his foot raised in the air, suspended, until it's time to lower it. Here the point of the dance is to find an elegant balance of expression. The foot, in the Sioux dance, is lowered only when the beat of the drum is heard, thus establishing a harmony between the drummer and the dancer. The art of the dance is to participate intelligently with the beat of the drum.

If you keep putting your foot down when there's no drumbeat, it's an indication that you're in distress. You're a clunker. You're clunking around, out of harmony, out of sync, with the rhythm of your life. Your pathetic prowess inelegantly puts your foot down at the wrong time.

For me, yoga has been a way to attain a certain elegance of balance in my life. In this I make no great claims, but I know as well as I know anything that yoga has helped me to function better than before. Before I discovered yoga, I used to feel unbalanced, uncentred, out of whack with my own inner, hidden life. In fact, for far too long I wasn't even aware that I even had an inner life. Certainly, nobody I knew in my twenties talked about this kind of thing.

This was true as well at theological seminary, where there was no attention paid to focused spiritual practices, such as meditation. I felt pressure then to be externally focused, and I didn't know how to turn within. Whenever I felt stressed, my habit was either to pace around the house or watch television. I didn't know then that by doing a few simple yoga postures, or by sitting for a while in meditation, I could radically alter my inner state.

Sister Edith Stein has written about how crucial it is to find this balanced elegance by engaging and establishing a harmony with your own hidden, inner life. In her book *The Hidden Life*, she writes that each of us has an "internal and individual structure."[18] And that internal and individual structure longs for self-expression.

Surely, according to the Sister, if we're to find some level of balance, it will depend on directing our attention to that hidden life. The life in fact that you are meant to live, according to Edith Stein, is written in your very nature. It is coded in your soul.

It is "particular and individual."[19]

That is, it is no one else's life.

It is your own.

Since that's the case, it's important to avoid importing images from outside yourself that don't fit who you are or ever will be. It's critical, says the wise Sister, to realize that you are "unique and unrepeatable."[20] She therefore warns: "Do not import and impose upon yourself foreign models that could squash your own individual traits and character."[21] Instead direct all your attention toward the discovery of your own hidden life, or higher life, and then live that out with every fibre of your being. And find, like the dancing Shiva, that you can rise in triumph.

George Faludy, like Sister Edith Stein, put his emphasis on finding your reason for being by following the dictates of your higher nature.[22] While a political prisoner, Faludy, to feed the souls of his fellow inmates, led them in the study of the great masterpieces of literature.

Though some responded, many mocked him. The scoffers said how foolish it was to waste valuable sleeping time on lectures and discussions!

Faludy then watched the scoffers, who ignored the needs of their higher natures. After a while, they withdrew into themselves and began to disintegrate, becoming "lonely and merciless" toward others.[23] And then he noticed that one by one these men would eventually walk off into the snow to die. These had been the ones, he said, who had been the most determined to survive and who, instead of caring for their spiritual needs, concentrated on nothing but food, sleep, and warmth.

Those who endured the camps were the ones who studied poetry and Plato's Socratic dialogues. Thus engaged, their spirits were strengthened, and the effect was to prevent the collapse of their bodies.

Addressing graduating students at the University of Toronto, in 1979, George Faludy concluded his address with these words: "Our whole fragile tradition of art and thought is neither an amusement nor a yoke. For those who steep themselves in it, it provides both a guide and a goal for surpassing all the half-baked ideologies that have blown up at our feet in this century like landmines."[24]

The point here is to emphasize the inestimable value of a daily practice of tending to the soul as one's top priority. Perhaps this can be done through a yoga/meditation practice or the study of the Bible, or of great works of literature and philosophy. It is through such means that we increase our chances of getting a little better at attaining a soulful, elegant balancing act instead of collapsing and disintegrating.

Chapter Four:
Thomas Merton and Me

A YOUNG MAN had been preparing for the United States Foreign Service at Georgetown University but with no enthusiasm. Bored, he called his focus then a "decent plan at the time for some sort of career in international affairs."[25] He was a long way from being in the grip of some passion or sense of call.

But everything was about to change.

It was because of a book.

It was Thomas Merton's *The Seven Storey Mountain*, the story of a young Columbia University intellectual who became a Christian and then a Roman Catholic monk. The book's impact was enormous. The young man writes:

> Never had words been so intimate to my own latent feelings, and never had their honesty and authenticity moved me so deeply. Merton's journey charted a path into my own heart, stirring questions I did not dare ignore. Indeed, as I finished the book, I felt an aliveness I had never known.[26]

That sense of "an aliveness I had never known" was the awakening of "a primal desire that would henceforth be a factor in every decision I would ever make, in every moment of self-discovery I would ever experience."[27]

That young man became Brother Christopher, a monk of some fifty years now. Brother Christopher is one of many who have been smitten by the life and writings of the Trappist monk, Thomas Merton. I, too, am a member of that club.

When I arrived for seminary studies in Kentucky in 1975, my first purchase was the book *New Seeds of Contemplation* by Thomas Merton. When my fiancée joined me a semester later, our first big date was a visit to the Abbey of Gethsemani in Bardstown, Kentucky, the monastery where Merton lived out his vocation until his death in 1968.

Two events stand out at the monastery. One was the discovery of The Thomas Merton room, where we were thrilled to hear a cassette tape of an animated Thomas Merton lecturing his students. I had not expected the abundance of energy and laughter! There was both depth and fun in the classroom. Merton was a captivating live wire, the opposite of anything dull or sour.

The second great event was to hear Gregorian chant for the first time. I was enchanted. Growing up Baptist, I had never heard anything like it. Ready for change, I thought, *I've been looking for this kind of music all my life!* A pianist, I have since played the chants I heard that day over and over until my hands ached.

Merton has thus been an inspiring point of reference many times along my life journey. A biography of Merton, by Monica Furlong, rates as a long-time favourite, along with *Thomas Merton's Dark Path* by William Shannon, which, when I read it, had the effect of removing a certain weight from my shoulders. It was the weight of the shallow certainties that tend to be characteristic of popular religion. I needed something deeper, but I didn't know it existed. But there it was in Merton's emphasis on what he called the *apophatic* way of knowing.

Merton gave me words for a deeper level of knowing that I had somehow known all my life without having ever heard anyone talk about it. This highly significant level of understanding feels paradoxically like a state of *not knowing*, yet this not knowing has more to it than anything else. It is, I think, that way of understanding that can be compared to what the Old Testament prophet Elijah experienced in the dark cave when he heard a still, small voice.[28] You can barely hear such a whisper in the dark, but it has more power to it than all flashy revelations.

It's this apophatic way of knowing—the way of not knowing—that's almost entirely absent in all expressions of popular religion. Since that's the case, I am constitutionally unable to walk in the door of a good many churches, for I immediately feel and am repulsed by the neon-light religiosity.

Not long ago, I read *The Asian Journal of Thomas Merton*. Merton's dream had been to travel to the Orient. Before boarding the plane, Merton—in characteristic Merton fashion—was required to pay extra for the over-load of books he carried. Ever the keen student, among the books was a copy of Herman Hesse's *Siddhartha*.

It was while in Asia that the most profound religious experience of Merton's life occurred. In Ceylon, Merton came upon several Buddhist statues:

> Looking at these figures I was suddenly, almost forcibly, jerked clean out of the habitual, half-tied vision of things, and an inner clearness, clarity, as if exploding from the rocks themselves, became evident and obvious. I don't know when in my life I have ever had such a sense of beauty and spiritual vitality running together in one aesthetic illumination.[29]

Concerning this Christian who experienced illumination in a Buddhist context, Amiya Chakravarty says: "Merton sought the fullness of man's inheritance; an inclusive view that made it impossible for him to deny any authentic scripture or any man of faith."[30] In other words, truth was truth for Merton, wherever it could be found.

Merton's was an open, searching spirit, a questing spirit—perhaps in short supply elsewhere. For what can too easily be found in contrast to Merton's spirit is *another spirit*, as I was alarmed to find in a book called *The Ladder of Divine Ascent* by St. John Climacus. Initially I found some value in what I read, especially in what Climacus had to say about going into exile. Climacus was compelling as he described the state of a spiritual exile as "an irrevocable renunciation of everything in one's familiar surroundings that hinders one from attaining the ideal of holiness."[31] That was all well and good. Also, captivating was when Climacus defined an exile as someone who has a "disciplined heart" and an "unpublicized understanding."[32] The exile, furthermore, engages in "unseen meditation," longs for what is "divine," lives with "an outpouring of love," and lives in "a depth of silence."[33]

All of this was very, very good!

But then came Step #5 on his Ladder of Ascent, the section titled "On Penitence." I paused and shuddered, for here was a spirit, an attitude, completely unlike Merton's. It was something else.

A different spirit.

An utterly repulsive spirit.

I found it disturbing, for example, to read about the month Climacus spent at a place called "The Monastery Prison." I cringed to read that Climacus appeared not only to have approved of but to have taken satisfaction in the self-tortures that the penitents endured there as they practised a most severe asceticism. Climacus presents the men of the monastery prison as *holy men* whose practices included torturing themselves so severely that

> Their knees were like wood, the result of all the prostrations. Their eyes were dim and sunken. Their hair was gone, and cheeks wasted, scalded by many tears. Their faces were pale and worn. They were no different from corpses.[34]

Climacus writes, apparently approvingly, that the men's "breasts were livid (black and blue) from all the beatings, which had even made them spit blood. There was no rest for them in their beds, no clean and laundered clothing. They were bedraggled, dirty and verminous."[35]

I was bothered enough to do some research and soon discovered a present-day fan of Climacus who says about the Step #5 section: "If there is any part of the book which really shakes us and brings the message home, it is precisely this chapter concerning those 'blessed inmates of the prison.'"[36] For, as he comments, "truly these are holy ones, crazed for Christ."[37]

I thought, *well, you got the crazy part right, but nothing else.*

As I kept up the research, I was relieved and delighted to find that Merton himself had read what I had and shared my revulsion. Merton was, I'm glad to report, blessedly out of touch with his inner Climacus. Merton's assessment mirrors mine, as he describes *The Ladder of Ascent* as "seldom, if ever tender—a tough, hard-hitting, merciless book." Concerning the goings-on at the monastery prison, Merton's evaluation is that it "reads today like a report of a badly-run mental institution."[38]

I then discovered that the contemporary fan of the abominable Step #5 section read about Merton's reaction and decided to go after Father Tom in the very spirit of the monastery prison! In a contemporary replication of that spirit, the devotee of Climacus lampooned Merton: "Merton travelled to the Far East, there to seek from the worshippers of demons new insights and techniques for finding God. And it is there that this hapless man, instead of finding God, found only his own tragic death."[39]

This sounds like the author is on the edge of suggesting that Merton got what he deserved for opening his heart to the Orient.

Merton, if you haven't heard, was electrocuted while in the Orient by a faulty fan as he stepped into a bathtub. When I first heard this, I wept in response.

There is the open, searching spirit of a Thomas Merton and then there is something else—a very different spirit. Scott Cairns, an Eastern Orthodox poet and literature professor, has cast light upon the difference between two very different spiritualities. That first spirit Cairns calls a "spirituality of the resurrection"; the second, a "spirituality of crucifixion."[40] Cairns characterizes the spirit of resurrection as "running towards something."[41] The contrasting "spirituality of crucifixion" is "running away from something."[42] The first spirit, says Cairns, has to do with "health and holiness, of a sense of joy already attained in God's kingdom." The second spirit Cairns calls "a species of hell."[43]

Well, it's one spirit or the other, and I'm with Merton's. Merton's spirit was all about a burning desire to know truth, beauty, and goodness. To feed that hunger, says Merton, you gather your attention toward the "pure truth" at the centre of your being:

> At the center of our being is a point of nothingness which is untouched by sin and by illusion, a point of pure truth, a point or spark which belongs entirely to God, which is ever at our disposal, and inaccessible to the fantasies of our mind or the brutalities of our own will. This little point of

nothingness and of absolute poverty is the pure glory of God in us. It is like a pure diamond, blazing with the invisible light of heaven. It is in everybody, and if we could see it, we would see these billion points of light coming together in the face and blaze of a sun that would make all the darkness and cruelty of life vanish completely.[44]

Merton's focus was upon the Light of the soul at the centre of our being. It is "the pure glory of God within us." To enter that sacred space is everything.

Chapter Five:
No Life Without Poetry

I VIVIDLY RECALL my late father-in-law, a businessman and great reader, spending his evenings sitting in an armchair and reading poetry, especially the poetry of T.S. Eliot. Comfortably situated, he would sit regularly amid a library of hundreds of books. In his bliss there, he was a member of a dying breed of classically oriented, high-minded gentlemen—the antithesis of those who squander their time in front of video games. It was clear for any visitor to this library sanctuary that before their eyes was an impressive class act, someone who truly had a life.

When I married his daughter, it was plain that I was marrying her father's daughter. For example, on our second date (after a philosophy lecture the night before), this blonde with brains arrived at my family's home with an armload of books. To the marriage, she brought shelves full of English literature and an ambition to teach literature and poetry. As my father-in-law was distinctive, so is his daughter.

An example of my father-in-law's distinctiveness was his proclivity to make resounding one-line declarations that would effectively close the case on any subject. One of these was: "There is no life without poetry." He made the point as if stating the obvious, expecting no dissent or discussion. The implication was that only a dullard would disagree. It was implied that you'd have to be stupid not to get such a self-evident point.

Al McGee

When he would deliver one of his one-line zingers, it was always with the power-packed punch of authority. Those of us standing around him were expected to realize that the final word on some matter had been spoken: "No argument. No discussion," he used to say. The case was now closed. He was setting forth some unarguable fact—in this case, the plain truth that there is no life without poetry, indicating his understanding that life is somehow incomplete, is missing something, when the poetic dimension is ignored.

He never explained why a life without poetry has no meaning. He never spelled it out for anyone, as far as I'm aware. It wasn't his way to talk about poetry directly. Instead, he simply read, memorized, and recited poetry. It was perhaps all too personal for him. Perhaps he felt that nobody would understand what he cared most about. And so, sequestered in his armchair, he kept it all to himself, privately tucked away.

That has always been my wife's understanding of her father's way, which was never to hear directly about what he loved. Instead, he communicated non-verbally, as my wife has often said, through his eyes. She always felt that theirs was a shared understanding of the supreme value of the poetic dimension. She could therefore relax in his presence, feeling known, loved, and understood—the assurance of those immeasurable gifts coming from the tenderness and understanding in his eyes.

It has been left for this father's daughter to give a public expression of the power of poetry in her high school literature classes. And thus, it is my wife's aim as an English teacher to awaken the poetic dimension in her students. This is to be in accord with the great American writer, Ralph Waldo Emerson, who said that the test of the poet is the "power to take the passing day, with its news, its cares, its fears," and to "hold it up to Divine reason" until the day is seen "to have a purpose and a beauty" and to see its relation to "the eternal order of the world."[45]

The task of the poet is, in other words, to facilitate an ascension into higher realms of meaning and experience, which is to participate in that felt understanding of things that has traditionally, for example, been the perspective of the mind of India—the understanding of "a universe permeated with immense purpose."[46] It is also, most critically and personally, to find that reality within you as your own true identity, your own higher consciousness. Upon awakening into that poetic realm, you then become increasingly drenched with an awareness of that Divine dimension to the point of saturation.

Someone who has felt this poetic dimension intensely told me once (with some anguish) that she had tried to describe her spiritual quest to her mother but was immediately shut down. Dear Mom didn't understand her daughter's searching ways and was baffled and confused by the intensity. Like not a few others, she simply didn't want to go *there* and was full of fear about any kind of emphasis on inner exploration. It wasn't her mother's way to inquire about entering new vistas that could open her up to truth and understanding.

The mother's way, as described by her daughter, was to get up and get going, but rarely, if ever, pausing to reflect on the meaning of it all. She never asked what it's all about. Life goes on happening, but the mother isn't in it with any kind of significant level of comprehension or understanding.

My sense is that lots of people, sad to say, may live out their days in just this kind of unreflective, unexamined way. They do a bunch of things.

Go a lot of places.

Make a lot of noise.

Then fade away.

This dismal way of living is about various noises being made—all kinds of grunts and sounds—like the discordant sounds of pots and pans being banged together, all amounting to but "a sound and a fury, signifying nothing."[47]

I used to hear such disturbing, discordant sounds at a nursing home where I served as a chaplain when the kitchen band performed. The residents were encouraged to bash pots and pans together while someone thumped on the piano the World War One soldiers' song, "It's a Long Way to Tipperary." I tell you; it was a foretaste of hell! The most deplorable of sights. And I shudder to think of it now. I used to think, is this the culminating point of a life well-lived, to end up a member of the kitchen band?

I have dared to hope for a gentler, quieter, more dignified exit from the planet. I entertain the wild hope that I will never be led shuffling down the hall of a nursing home to take my place in some kitchen band ensemble. I'd prefer to be taken out early by a drone than to suffer such a fate. I'd like a quick death rather than ever join the ranks of some hell-bound kitchen band. Perhaps if I enter the poetic realm enough, I'll build up enough inner strength so that, however frail my condition, I'll have the strength to scream at some kitchen band recruiter, "Get away from me!"

Thus, concerned about my fate, my practice is to enter that poetic, deeper dimension of things and to remain established there. Jacob Needleman describes this as the appearance of "I am" in one's life. He describes this experience as unique: "Here, now, I exist—a feeling like no other emotion in our lives."[48] Needleman writes of "those moments, when we are touched by the appearance in ourselves of a very fine presence that seems a mysterious homecoming: 'I am here. I am home.'"[49] This is a felt shift from an ordinary, everyday level of awareness to an awareness of the Divine presence. Most deeply, says Needleman, it is a breakthrough into a sense that "I am seen, loved and understood. I am being seen by something higher than myself. Of being seen by the Higher. Known by the Higher. Being loved."[50]

This is poetry at its highest level.

This sense of "I am" is the result of a struggle for true being. That level of true being is the experience of when my "thoughts, desires and sensations are inhabited"[51] by the embrace of the spiritual dimension. Such a level of profound experience and the quality of struggle required to find it is, says Needleman, almost "unknown in the loud world."[52]

The search for the "I am, I am home" experience is almost entirely absent, "completely unknown in almost all the religion, art and science of the blind world."[53]

But the "I am, I am home" experience of the poetic dimension doesn't have to be foreign. We can choose emphatically to assert with my father-in-law that "There is no life without poetry."

And we can resolve to create a life that is packed full of the poetic dimension and spirit.

I repeat for emphasis—life is somehow incomplete—is missing something, when the poetic dimension—the dimension of soul—is ignored.

Chapter Six:
It's All Good? Oh, C'mon!

I HAD JUST received a fabulous job offer. It was a dream come true. I told a dear friend about it, a Roman Catholic Sister, whose habit of mind was always to penetrate to the heart of any matter. That's what I liked about her—her laser-like ability to see into the essence of things.

I fully expected her to discern with me that I was on track with this job offer. But, lo and behold, she didn't see in that way, and she unleashed upon me the fullness of her discriminating powers by asking a completely disarming question: "What's the shadow side of your adventure?"

Shadow side? Shadow side? I hadn't heard that phrase before. And I didn't want to. I gulped and inwardly thought, *what do you mean by shadow side?* Why the suggestion of menacing shadows? Why this negativity? Why so unhopeful? Why so pessimistic? How about "Congratulations, Al," as in "Way to go, Al! Good on you, mate!"

What kind of friend challenges you to look at the worst thing about an exciting job prospect? The best kind of friend, I was later able to affirm—the kind of friend who wants you to look squarely at every aspect of something, lest you walk in unaware. It's the best kind of friend, who encourages you to keep looking without flinching. (One's best friend may not be the one who too quickly starts pouring champagne!)

All I was thinking was that it was the best job ever! How could there be a shadow side to something so, so good? This job offer stood out as the answer to all my hopes and prayers. But it was my very certainty, as the Sister was discerning, that was the problem.

She knew that I was too much basking in the light and not wanting to think about lions and tigers and bears. To shake me a little, the Sister, highly intuitive and well trained in Jungian psychology, was imploring me to look at the dark side of the venture. Her point was to suggest that there's always a dark side, a shadow side. There's always something you'd rather not notice, something you'd rather not be aware of.

The Sister discerned that my desire was for light only; I was therefore lost in the light and blinded by it. My very sense of light was blocking me from noticing the dark side of the alluring prospect.

My choice to ignore her advice and remain stubbornly in the light by accepting the job prospect ensured that I would walk straight into the darkest of pits. And it took a while to dig out. Yet my experience in the dark pit has served to create a bigger theology and a greater psychology. It has become clear to me that any way of thinking that excludes the darkness is not only incomplete but dangerous.

You cannot insist upon summer all year long. Such a stance will blind and paralyze you—maybe not right away, but eventually, for sure. You will surely fall if you, for example, try to live only in the light of Easter without also acknowledging the darkness of Lent. However great your experience of light, you must be aware that a capacity for darkness remains (Pride cometh …).

Considering this experience (and others too), I have become allergic to excessively positive and hopeful claims from overly sunny people. I don't believe for a moment those who claim they have entirely overcome the darkness with the light. I'm suspicious of any who imagine that in them no darkness remains. I've been in their state of denial and want never to go there again.

When Soul Appears

I am wary of people who are a little too sunny and smiley, who are quick to claim, "It's all good." For it's never all good in this life. If you think so, you may be lying to yourself. I cringe a little when someone says, "It's all good!" This means I do a fair bit of cringing, since this is many people's favourite saying these days.

My question: Is it all good?

Well, yes, in some ultimate sense. Julian of Norwich declares that, finally: "All shall be well, and all manner of thing shall be well."[54] But for now, in this moment, all good? I don't think so. Sorry.

It's only all good if you're not quite living on the planet but floating in space somewhere.

As you say, "It's all good," you're probably not thinking about the parents of the young man who received, one by one, their son's chopped-off fingers in the mail from ISIS. Before you say again, "It's all good," you might pause for a moment to contemplate the severed fingers arriving in the mail. You might, in other words, wake up and shake yourself a little, for it's not all good.

The lesson here is to challenge yourself to be aware that the sunny script you're following requires a certain delicate balancing act with a darker script. Even if you've found the best script ever to live by you must also simultaneously imagine a contradicting counter-script. No matter how great your dream, your best-laid plan, you need to be aware as well of possible nightmare scenarios. So wisely determine to put as much energy into imagining the worst as you do the best.

But we don't want to think the worst. We don't want to consider contradicting counter-scripts or nightmarish dimensions, so we become peppy and cheery to cover it up. But the cover-up never works. We'll never be able entirely to dispense with the darkness. It's too powerful a force.

The shadow remains as a dynamic force and doesn't take to being ignored. But you, sweet thing, don't think so! No monster lurks within you?

A better way was demonstrated by the leadership of James Burke, the chief executive officer of Johnson & Johnson, the makers of Tylenol. He had been worrying about how the company would respond if something went wrong. He was, in the terms of this chapter, exploring the shadow side of the company. In 1979, he got his staff together to focus on the company's credo. The credo was a list of principles to live by, including their "higher duty to mothers and all others who use our products."[55] The credo, with its emphasis on a "higher duty," was the company script. But was it still being followed? Was there a danger of contradicting scripts taking over?

Challenging the company's leaders, he exclaimed, "If we're not going to live by the Credo, let's tear it off the wall."[56] After much discussion, everyone decided to resuscitate the credo. It's good that they did, for less than three years later, the news reported that people had been poisoned by Tylenol capsules in Chicago. Without hesitating, and in accordance with the credo's emphasis on a higher duty, all bottles of Tylenol were removed from store shelves everywhere. In doing this, the company took a hundred-million-dollar loss but kept their reputation. I love this tidbit from the story: "Burke, in fact, was on a plane when news of the poisoning broke. By the time he landed, employees were already ordering Tylenol off store shelves."[57]

By anticipating problems, problems were averted.

In contrast is the case of the *Challenger* space-shuttle disaster, where problems were not anticipated. The shadow was ignored. The pressuring script at NASA was to launch the *Challenger* on time. As problems came up (and they did), they were ignored. The consequence? The *Challenger* exploded several seconds after liftoff.

So, is it all good? No. Not all of it. Some of it, yes.

When Soul Appears

The point is to have a vision but to be aware of its shadow side.

Ever so aware.

Chapter Seven:
A Horror of Confinement

IT WAS SAID about the poet Rainer Maria Rilke that he had a horror of anything confined. This is to feel as if everything is closing in on you and that no escape is possible. Says Rilke:

> It feels as though I make my own way through massive rock. Like a vein of ore, alone, encased. I am so deep inside it; I can't see the path or any distance. Everything is close, and everything closing in on me has turned to stone.[58]

Feeling so confined, Rilke has lost all perspective and lives with a terrible darkness.

And yet, while feeling almost hopelessly smothered, another feeling arises. Perhaps against all odds and all hope, there is some longing, a yearning for transcendence, that presents itself. It's a yearning deep and strong for a higher or deeper dimension beyond the limits of his mind and senses. The poet senses that a mysterious force, call it God, the Absolute, or the Ultimate, is reaching down to spring him free. And so, he prays, and he does so in personal terms. He isn't praying to some vague, impersonal force but has rather a perception of the Divine as personal: "If it's You, press down hard on me, break in that I may know the weight of your hand and you, the fullness of my cry."[59]

He thus perceives the Divine not as oppressive weight to be cast off but as a power to embrace. He wants more of this power, not less. He's not losing his religion but finding it. A surge of hope arises that God is reaching into his painful enclosure to lift him up into a domain of unlimited space and freedom.

Rilke understands that it's not religion but everything else—the world, his ego, his troubles of whatever kind—that are closing in on him. He's not searching for the peace that the world can give—which is no peace at all, as Jesus said—but that peace that comes from an encounter with the One who is reaching down to save him.

I was twenty years old when I woke with a start from a nightmare, trembling with fear. I had dreamed that I was lying on a board, and I had no arms or legs. A harsh, mocking voice whispered, "I have you." I had never felt more terrified or hopeless. It was my experience, like Rilke's, of feeling entirely closed in and without hope.

That nightmare was a revelation of the state I was then in. The message was, "This is how your life is, Al. You're in a state of confinement because your soul is barren." It was the perception of a deep inner lack at the heart of me, a painfully revealing glimpse of the quality of my life.

Mine was a life, pathetically, almost totally dependent on the game of basketball. But now, as an immobile trunk, how would I find meaning? What meaning is there if life has only a physical dimension to it? If I couldn't score hoops, what would keep me going? I had the distinct feeling that if life has a point, I surely was missing it.

Because of that nightmare and the sense that I, like Rilke, was being reached out to from another dimension, the focus of my life changed entirely. I became vitally and urgently concerned about grounding my life in a spiritual dimension. I started going to church. I started to pray. I started to read books by C.S. Lewis, beginning with his masterpiece, *The Great Divorce*. I was beginning to break free.

Rilke, in his *Letters to a Young Poet*, with great hopefulness wrote that it is possible to break out of whatever weight is closing in upon us. We can deepen our sense of the Divine through the practice of solitude. It is through solitude, he says, that we can enter that other dimension—the kingdom of God—which is there as a sacred space of unlimited immensity: "Only one thing is necessary, and that is solitude—the immense inward solitude—to withdraw into oneself and not to meet anyone for hours."[60]

Rilke affirms that we can experience a vital connection with that One, anterior to the mind and senses, who can be experienced as a liberating force, regardless of how great the pressure may be upon us. It is possible through an encounter with the Divine to experience what Rilke calls an indestructible intimacy:

> Put out my eyes; I can see thee. stop up my ears; I can hear thee, and without feet I can go to thee, and without a mouth I can still call upon thee. Tear off my arms, and I shall yet seize thee with my heart as with a hand. Stop my heart, my brain will go on beating. and if thou settest fire to my brain, I shall still bear thee in my blood.

That indestructible intimacy is a heightened state of consciousness. To be in it, Rilke exclaims, "there is a tremendous solitude. How freely one breathes!"[61] And how clearly one thinks! In that transcendent realm of space and freedom is "the silent peak of true cognition."[62] In other words, such a contemplative state is the highest reach of human intelligence. Rilke encourages his readers to plumb the depths of the "furthest possible reach of the heart."[63] This is the inner journey that Fr Henri Le Saux called the "ascent to the depth of the heart," which is to experience the "unbounded spaciousness of the heart."[64] It is to experience a sense of intimacy with the energy of light and love that is the deepest ground of your own being and all of life.

There is a way out of the horror of confinement. It is to respond to that hand that reaches down to raise you up from the darkness of confinement.

I thank God for the self-revealing nightmare.

Chapter Eight: Seeing With or Through the Eye?

I HAVE LONG admired the British journalist, Malcolm Muggeridge, who in the 1970s was the most well-known journalist in the world. I have two shelves (often consulted) full of his books. One of these, *A Third Testament*, introduced me to his mentor, the poet William Blake, and his insight that to see *with* rather than *through* the eye is to render we humans vulnerable to propaganda and lies. In Blake's words: "We ever must believe a lie / When we see 'with,' not 'through' the eye."[65] If the powers of your soul are blocked or disabled, you will "see without seeing." You'll look at this or that but miss its meaning.

Blake's message is that our ability to see and understand depends upon whether something inside of us, an inner faculty of awareness, is sufficiently charged to enable clear seeing and understanding. It is therefore of the utmost importance as we look around that we see through our physical eyes by way of an awakened inner spiritual dimension.

To see with the eye only is to see without soul. In such a condition, we may be like the tourists Thomas Merton once described, who took many camera shots of paintings at an art gallery without ever understanding the meaning of any of them.[66] In other words, the tourists were themselves seeing mechanically, like their own cameras.

Merton's approach, in contrast, was to activate the powers of his soul by gathering his attention to focus on just one painting for a sustained period. He was then seeing through his eyes by the powers of his own soul.

The teaching of the great sages and seers has always been that our ability to see and understand, which is to discern what matters and what doesn't, depends upon the inner awakening of our souls' capacities. This is the awakening of an inner faculty of awareness that has been called *the mind's eye* or *the eye of the soul*. What's distinctive about seers is that they are fully lit up from within.

Their souls have been turned on.

Their psychic depths have been awakened.

A seer's mind's eye, or eye of the soul, has been ignited.

In a saint, the mind's eye is on fire!

When that inner faculty of perception is aroused, we're able to see through the physical eyes into the meaning of things.

The inability to see and understand is illustrated by a story Muggeridge once told. He tells of a "very humane, but simple-minded old lady who saw the play *King Lear* performed and was outraged that the poor old man should be humiliated and made to suffer."[67] As she watched the play, she directed her attention to only one surface fact—the suffering of the poor old man. If there was more to the play, she didn't take it in, for she had stopped short of exploring whether there was anything more to the play than what she didn't want to see! As the story goes, the woman was given the chance to question Shakespeare in the afterlife:

'What a monstrous thing,' she exclaimed to Shakespeare, 'to make that poor old man go through all of that.' 'Why, yes,' said Shakespeare, 'I quite agree. It was very painful, and I could have arranged for him to take a sedative at the end of Act 1, but then, ma'am, there would have been no play.'[68]

Because she was seeing with her physical eyes only, unaided by an activated inner life, she missed the play's main point, which was the salvific role of suffering. Having put a filter over the eye of her soul, she couldn't comprehend the meaning of the play and had missed its main point.

According to Malcolm Muggeridge's biographer, Ian Hunter, Muggeridge's special ability, his gift, was to see through the eye and thereby grasp the meaning that others missed. It had long been his practice to see through surfaces to the heart and depths of things. As he wrote in *A Twentieth Century Testimony*:

> I feel as though all my life I've been searching for an alternative scene, for the face behind the cotton wool, the flesh beneath the wax, the light beyond the arc lights, time beyond the ticking of the clocks, a vista beyond the furthermost reach of mortal eyes, for a destiny beyond history. I've always had the feeling from my earliest memories, that somehow, somewhere there was another dimension of reality where the fancy dress was put aside, the great paint was washed off, the arc lights were lowered.[69]

Muggeridge was ever sure that there is always more going on than what meets the physical eye. Yet as a child, Malcolm had been indoctrinated into a truncated way of looking at the world. He was taught to look at it through a socialistic lens. He wasn't taught to understand and accept that the world is full of both joy and woe, but rather that all "woe" could be banished by the advent of a socialist utopia.

Muggeridge recalls "the little suburban house in south London, where on Saturday evenings my father and his cronies would assemble, and they would plan together the downfall of the capitalist system and the replacement of it by one which was just and human and egalitarian and peaceable etc."[70] Malcolm had then

> accepted completely the views of these good men, that once they were able to shape the world as they wanted it to be, they would create a perfect state of affairs in which peace would reign, prosperity would expand, men would be brotherly, and considerate, and there would be no exploitation of man by man, not any ruthless oppression of individuals.[71]

The trouble was that it was all a lie, as he would discover for himself upon being assigned to Moscow in the early 1930s. He'd been sent there by the *Manchester Guardian* newspaper, which he mockingly described as that "high citadel of liberalism" where "the truth was being expounded, where enlightenment reigned." These, he exclaimed, "were the golden days of liberalism when the *Guardian* was widely read, and even believed!"[72]

The aim of the newspaper wasn't so much about seeing and understanding the truth of things, but to spread socialist propaganda.

Muggeridge found in Moscow that he could no longer subscribe to the leftist vision as he watched with disgust the "extraordinary performance of the liberal intelligentsia, who, in those days, flocked to Moscow like pilgrims to Mecca." He saw that one and all were utterly delighted and excited by what they saw there: Clergymen walked serenely and happily through the anti-God museums, politicians claimed that no system of society could possibly be more equitable and just, lawyers admired Soviet justice, and economists praised the Soviet economy.[73]

Alarmed, Muggeridge asked, "How could this be? How could this extraordinary credulity exist in the minds of people who were adulated by one and all as maestros of discernment and judgment?"[74]

He answered by contrasting the blindness of the Western clergy, politicians, and lawyers with the spiritual insight gained by the prisoners of "the forced labor camps of the USSR,"[75] among whom was the former communist, Alexander Solzhenitsyn. Solzhenitsyn emerged from the Gulag with the spiritual message, "Bless you prison … for there I came to realize that the object of life is the maturity of the human soul."[76] The object of life, according to Solzhenitsyn, is to acquire the Spirit, to attain the spiritual perspective—the very thing the Soviets had tried to suppress.

For reporting the truth about the Soviet prison camps, Malcolm Muggeridge lost his job at the *Guardian* and was blacklisted far and wide. He was cancelled for choosing to see soulfully *through* the eye rather than *with* the eye. Muggeridge is therefore a model of a true seer, able to see clearly because of an activated soul and conscience.

Chapter Nine: Frightfully Normal

THE PROBLEM WITH being normal, according to Colin Wilson, is that to be normal is to be in a depressed condition. In Wilson's terms, to be normal is to be dimly aware, to be in an impoverished state, falling woefully short of what you're capable of becoming. If the extent of your awareness is a mere everyday level of awareness, you ought not to trust yourself, for as Wilson states, "Ordinary consciousness is a liar."[77] You cannot trust that in such an ordinary, limited state you can know what's true and what matters.

Your ordinariness may perhaps get you by, but in such a semi-conscious frame of mind, you'll never know the heights, depths, and joy of higher levels of consciousness.

Bruce Charlton agrees: "It was forty years ago that Colin Wilson made me recognize explicitly something I had unconsciously felt for about five years, which was that ordinary everyday human consciousness is essentially worthless." He explains: "A life lived at that level is not really being lived—it is merely automatic behavior."[78]

The ordinary state, or state of the natural, average man, is a severely shackled condition. To be in such a limited state of consciousness is, according to Wilson, to be "frightfully normal." And to be frightfully normal is to be frightfully clueless.

Perhaps one of the chief characteristics of the frightfully normal human being is to go around being vacuously cheerful, trying to give everyone the impression that you are someone who always looks on the bright side of things (at least in public). On display is a mentality that exudes a certain kind of hopefulness, which upon being examined is shown to be counterfeit. What's exposed is a groundless, shallow optimism without substance or depth.

Typically, this ankle-deep attitude tends blithely and ignorantly to skate along on the surface of things without considering any shadows or darkness. Accordingly, it can be the dimmest of wits who seem to be falsely hopeful about this or that. If you try to pin down one of these dreamy types in terms of facts or evidence, they will quickly slip away from you, well-practised as they are at slip, slip, slip-sliding away from understanding the multi-dimensionality of what is.

The opposite of this dreamy mentality is the substance, depth, and coherence I saw in the American journalist, Whitelaw Reid, who, as an elderly gentleman, was interviewed during the World War Two documentary, *Finest Hour*.[79] In some eighteen snippets from the film, Mr. Reid comes across as a man of radiant conviction, clarity, and humour, grounded in the fullness of reality. His presence is palpable and mesmerizing.

As a young journalist, Whitelaw Reid had travelled to England to cover the Blitz of London by the Nazis (July 10 to October 1940). Then only twenty-six, Reid's task was to deliver daily reports from London as the bombs fell and London burned. That zone of horror had its effect on the young Whitelaw Reid, as it was there that he encountered the stark reality of Nazi savagery, which he described as "the demonic force of absolute evil."[80] His response to London's nightmare—this graduate in sociology from Yale University—was to conclude that "Hitler was an evil that had to be eliminated."[81]

When Reid returned to America, he went on the warpath against Hitler, writing articles and giving talks on the specific theme that there are worse things than war. What's worse than war, said Mr. Reid, was to do nothing against tyranny and thereby allow the collapse of Great Britain. Reid knew that America had the resources to turn the tide against the Nazis, so he argued against the do-nothing isolationists, urging America to join the fight against evil.

In my estimation, Reid is an exemplar of what it means to be a human being in full, that is, fully aware, and anything but frightfully normal. He had a certain kind of understanding of human nature as being fully aware of the existence of two opposing tendencies, or capacities, that exist within us all.

On the one hand, a part of us has the potential to be far worse than can be comfortably contemplated, which is to be capable of levels of depravity and acts of horror beyond comprehension. On the other hand, there's a part, always to be considered, that has to do with the potential we each possess to be greater than has been thought humanly possible!

You and I are thus capable, according to this view of human nature, of becoming either everlasting horrors or everlasting splendours. We are, daily, moving in one or the other of these directions. To be fully aware is to be always considering both humanity's potential for wickedness and its potential for sainthood. When there is an emphasis only upon humanity's sunny prospects—a shallow wistfulness—the effect is to muddle the mind.

If you and I are living the normal life, which Colin Wilson calls the frightfully normal life, it means that we are succeeding at resigning ourselves to commonplace aspirations, which over time will inevitably result in a dim-eyed and undiscerning existence. If our desire is to attain insight and understanding, then we must indeed break out of the frightfully normal condition.

We must be like Celia, for example, a character in T.S. Eliot's *The Cocktail Party*, who has had more than enough of normal life and longs for a singularly meaningful one. The psychiatrist, Reilly, describes to Celia the frightfully normal condition of many people who may remember the vision they had, but they cease to regret it, maintain themselves by the common routine, learn to avoid excessive expectation, become tolerant of themselves and others. Giving and taking, in the usual actions what there is to give and take. They do not repine. Are contented with the morning that separates and with the evening that brings together for casual talk before the fire. Two people who know they do not understand each other, breeding children whom they do not understand and who will never understand them.[82]

People like these leave Celia cold. She cannot comprehend their satisfaction with what they are. She yearns instead for a life that is in touch with the energy of the soul. Celia determines to leave the frightfully normal condition behind to find instead a blessedly uncommon existence.

And she does.

Chapter Ten: Truly Educated

IT IS WITH a sense of wonder that from time to time I meet someone whose penchant is a certain readiness to get up and turn around—as in Plato's "Allegory of the Cave" where the unchained prisoner rises to turn toward the Light.

This movement of getting up to turn around is never the common thing to do.

The usual thing is to go on sitting there like an unthinking blob.

The usual thing is to drift.

The usual thing is an indifferent shrug of the shoulders.

The usual thing is a vacant stare into space.

The usual thing is to be on the go without pausing to reflect.

But the one who is consistently determined to get up to turn around, whose orientation is toward the Light, has had enough of the darkness of cave life. She's had more than enough of the soul-smothering entertainments of the cave dwellers. She hates how they spend their time, for she's caught a glimpse of something higher beyond the cave. And it's with a growing sense of alarm that she feels the necessity to get up to turn around before it's too late.

She's been thinking that some radical action is required, and now the impulse can no longer be denied or resisted.

And so, as the story goes, the seeker comes into that Light beyond the Cave and is lit up by it. Now immersed in the Light, a soul on fire, she begins to see by that Light, which means that she sees more clearly and loves more dearly than ever before. Sun-drenched, she has acquired a new perspective, a new understanding. Enlightened, she has become sharply delineated from what she was and now sees the stark difference between living in the Light or living in the darkness.

It is a knowledge that is almost more than she can bear. This level of knowing nearly tears her apart. In one sense, it was easier not to know. Now that she knows, it's both liberating and painful. But now that she has tasted eternity, there is no going back, whatever the cost.

In her illumined state, she now understands why *The Upanishads* admonish human beings to discern the difference between the unreal and the real. She now *gets* that we are called to choose between appearances and reality, to distinguish between living a surface life or a life of depth. Having emerged from the shadows into the Light, she now cares only to become more established in that which is substantial and enduring.

She is no longer a scoffer or a mocker. She is rather a searcher, a person with an open heart, not a closed one. Accordingly, while the crowd goes one way, she goes the other. While the crowd goes downstream because it's easy and fun—destined for the rapids—she swims upstream against the current, toward the promised land.

The proverb asks: "How long will scoffers delight in their scoffing and fools hate knowledge?"[83] The answer is that you never know. You don't know how long someone will remain unchanged and immovable. You don't know how long the skepticism will last. For some, it may be an entire lifetime of mocking and scoffing, resulting finally in a jaded and cynical state of psychological and spiritual impairment. The long-term damage of cynicism is a cold look on the face that scares off little children and small animals.

But there's another look! It's the look of someone who has resolutely remained in a state of wonder. Such an enchanted one, in Platonic terms, is the definition of a truly educated person, someone who has long cultivated the ability to perceive what Plato called the Beatific vision, the vision of the Beautiful.

Unlike the uneducated scoffer or mocker, Plato's educated person has been carefully cultivating the ability to discern the presence of that Divine, ultimate reference point at the heart of all things. By making it her constant practice to stand up to turn toward the Light, she has become able to know.

And that's the key word—*able*. To see clearly doesn't come easily or naturally, so to know fully depends on the intensity of one's longing and resolve. If you're looking for love in all the wrong places but not in the direction of the Light, you will never know anything worth knowing. You'll be like the mass of the population—lost in a lost world, forever bound, chained and gagged by constant distractions and diversions, the shadows on the wall of Plato's cave.

Evelyn Waugh tells of a classics teacher in a private school whose sole concern was to create just such "truly educated" and "complete" human beings. He is, in other words, a true teacher, for his desire is to bring his students out of the darkness into the Light. In Platonic terms, the classics teacher knows that it's his duty to prepare his students to behold the Beatific vision—the vision of the Highest.

But the school's headmaster, tragically, has decided that it's no longer important to teach the classics. Lacking vision, the headmaster has come to regard the classics as irrelevant and useless.

Addressing the classics teacher, the headmaster says:

> What are we to do? Parents aren't interested in producing the 'complete man' anymore. They want to qualify their boys for jobs in the modern world. You can hardly blame them, can you?
>
> Oh yes, I can and do.
>
> …Has it ever occurred to you that a time may come when there will be no more classical boys at all?
>
> Oh yes. Often.
>
> What I was going to suggest was—I wonder if you will consider taking some other subject as well as the classics? History, for example, preferably economic history.
>
> No, headmaster.
>
> But you know, there may be something of a crisis ahead.
>
> Yes, headmaster.
>
> Then what do you intend to do?

If you approve, headmaster, I will stay here as long as any one boy wants to read the classics. I think it would be a very wicked thing indeed to do anything to fit a boy for the modern world.

It's a short-sighted view.

There, Headmaster, with all respect, I differ from you profoundly. I think it is the most long-sighted view it is possible to take.'[84]

The classics teacher thus remained true to the *long-sighted view* of the true educator.

Chapter Eleven:
The Incommunicable Want

GREAT SEERS AND sages have often referred to a holy longing or desire with which we are born. This built-in want is hard to describe. C.S. Lewis called it incommunicable.

And yet, when it's there, you know it! And you'll try to write and talk about it, as Lewis did, even as words fail, for it is unmistakable in its power and force.

In a *Seinfeld* episode, Kramer asks George Costanza if he ever experienced deep yearning.

"George, have you ever yearned, like, really yearned?"

George sits scratching his head. "Yearning? Yearning? No, don't think I've ever yearned. I've craved. I've craved. I've really craved."

That's the difference between two very different kinds of feeling.

To crave has to do with something like craving pizza, or Tim Hortons donuts, or perhaps attention. But there's a feeling far greater and deeper than craving. It is to yearn with all your heart for the Highest, for the Ultimate, for God.

To share this vital and incomparable holy yearning with another is to ground your relationship in the strongest of foundations.

Fr Henri Le Saux said that this holy yearning "cannot be in anything that can be seen, heard touched or known in this world."[85]

In other words, it's a longing for another realm or dimension.

It's a longing for Transcendence.

A longing for the Divine.

A taste for the Infinite.

A sense of eternity in the heart.

A fire burning in the heart.

"I felt my heart strangely warmed,"[86] said John Wesley, the founder of the Methodists, and he was never the same again.

When two people are truly in love, they nurture this feeling for transcendence in each other. Think of a couple at the base of a triangle. As they listen to and love each other, they reinforce each other's deepest convictions, and both are elevated toward the triangle's peak—the eternal dimension. They are raising each other toward union with God.

C.S. Lewis perhaps said it best:

> Are not all lifelong friendships born at the moment when
> you at last meet another human being who has some inkling
> (but faint and uncertain even in the best) of that something

which you were born desiring, and which, beneath the flux of other desires and in all the momentary silences between the louder passions, night and days, year by years, from childhood to old age, you are looking for, watching for, listening for? You have never had it. All the things that have ever deeply possessed your soul have been but hints of it—tantalising glimpses, promises never quite fulfilled, echoes that died away just as they caught your ear. But if it should really become manifest—if there ever came an echo that did not die away but swelled into the sound itself—you would know it. Beyond all possibility of doubt, you would say 'Here at last is the thing I was made for.' We cannot tell each other about it. It is the secret signature or each soul, the incommunicable and unappeasable want, the thing we desired before we met our wives or made our friends or chose our work, and which we shall still desire on our deathbeds, when the mind no longer knows wife or friend or work. While we are, this. If we lose this, we lose all.[87]

Lewis thought this holy yearning so important that he emphasized that to lose it is to lose everything.

The message is at all costs to keep your own inner fire burning—with all your heart, soul and might.

Chapter Twelve: What Little I Know

I LIVE WITH a sense of God that I can barely explain.

About this sense of the Divine, I pause …

I hesitate …

I stammer and stutter …

For there is much I do not understand. I am painfully aware that my experience is limited and my knowledge partial. My experience is like St Paul's, who wrote that he sees as if through a glass darkly, and like the Irish poet/philosopher John O'Donohue, who pondered the difference between candlelight knowing and neon-light knowing. Like O'Donohue, I'm a candlelight knower and always ill at ease with the flashy certainties of neon-light spiritualities. Yet the little I know—a rare candle flickering in the dark—means everything to me.

I feel backed up and supported by Nicholas of Cusa, who in the fifteenth century wrote of the Christian as someone who "knows he cannot comprehend the Divine."[88] This limited knowing on the Christian's part—his posture of incomprehension—is, according to Nicholas, an indication of humility and openness before God. Such a not knowing, says Nicholas, is to be understood as a "necessary learned ignorance."[89]

Nicholas makes the point that the Christian's learned ignorance is wholly at odds with some pagan's certainty about what he thinks he knows. There is, I think, a choice to be made between these two incompatible positions—one that humbly knows a little, and one that perhaps arrogantly thinks it knows a lot.

I know that I wouldn't for a moment trade away the little I know for what the chesty pagan thinks he knows. I am repeatedly astonished to find that my very inability to comprehend opens the space for a greater knowledge to arise.

It's almost automatic in my experience that, when my mind calms, the spirit rises.

And I'm in a different place.

A better place.

A place that sets me free with a sense of new life arising.

When Spirit rises, I feel myself to be in a sacred space of barely knowing anything, but I find refreshingly in that state that something deeper is awakened. I find myself awakening to a higher or deeper level of knowing, participating in a level of knowing that transcends the intellect. I can affirm that "in Him, I live, move and have my being."[90]

Consequently, I no longer feel alone. In that luscious zone of experience, I am no longer standing apart from reality—thinking about it, analyzing it, or commenting on it. Rather, I'm in it. Instead of having thoughts about this or that, I have a sense that I am being thought. That, somehow, I am being expressed.

It may sound strange to say, but it's natural and wonderful to experience. In moments of illumination, I feel that I'm being expressed by a force greater than myself. I have a sense of being thought, of being in the mind of God and, in some sense, a thought of God. The experience is palpable and liberating. Nothing compares to it.

On that plane of experience, I am no longer outside of things, but inside. No longer looking at God, but inside of God. I'm in another zone, a greater space or realm, that Jesus called the "Kingdom of God."

I think it was this level of transcendental experience that St. Augustine had in mind when he exclaimed, in his Confessions: "You were more inward to me than my most inward part and higher than my highest."[91] Augustine's enlightened state involved a greater awareness of the Spirit than of his own self-awareness. In such a realm—a heightened state of consciousness—the believer is transported above both senses and the intellect. Located there, he or she senses that "old things are passed away and behold, all things become as new."[92] For anyone who has been there, which is to be lost in wonder, love, and praise, everything changes.

Someone commented, "Life begins when we tap into this level of knowledge. Till that time, we just exist." Till that time, we may, in other words, be just surviving, getting by. Putting in time.

Life begins when this deeper, higher reality is accessed, as streams of living water begin to gurgle and gush forth. It's the grand alternative to being dried up and depressed.

Who understands this?

Anyone?

Who can I tell this to?

Al McGee

Who cares?

All around me is noise.

The noise of the world—clashing, banging, booming.

People jostling for attention.

Non-stop chatter and arguments about nothing of consequence.

The discordant sounds are coming from people who are living in what they call their real world.

But it doesn't feel real to me.

It feels rather fake and false.

And more like living in a prison.

And indeed, it's killing them …

Their reality is killing them.

As someone confessed to me with amazing honesty, "What I live with all the time is the unceasing chatter of my own mind." Forever restless, she said, she can no longer sit to read a book, and would never try to meditate. So, she remains in her noisy, restless world, accompanied by a constantly chattering monkey-mind.

That is her *real* world.

It holds no interest for me. I come away from this and other empty encounters with a greater sense that I am perhaps on to something.

When Soul Appears

Something good.

What little I know ... an incomparable treasure.

Chapter Thirteen: Enduring Love

AN ANCIENT TALE by Ovid in his *Metamorphoses*—retold by Jacob Needleman in his book *The Wisdom of Love*—features a married couple whose names were Baucus and Philemon. It's a tale rarely noticed because there's no great drama to it. The usual attention-getters are frenzied stories of great passion that blaze out, like shooting stars that flash by and are gone. Here's a quieter story.

It's like the discovery of a faint star from which a subtle light is emitted—suggestive of another kind of reality, another kind of love.[93] It's a less sensational story about a deeper kind of love, a lasting love, a story that answers the question: What enables love to endure? Is there some mysterious secret that makes love last?

No. Like all best things, it is simple.

The simple thing that made the marriage of Baucus and Philemon work was the quality of attention they gave to each other. They listened to each other and grew old. Just how wild and crazy is that?

This may be the greatest gift that can be given—to listen and really hear! When someone truly listens to you and gives you his undistracted, undivided attention—when he is fully and palpably present, you feel loved. This level of listening is interpreted as love.

It's the greatest thing ever. To listen. And then to listen some more. To listen so well that you hear in her what she hasn't heard in herself. You catch her by surprise with how well you hear her, and how clearly you see her.

This quality of listening has been described in many ways, but I like the way Irish poet, W.B. Yeats described the nature of deep listening. He called it listening for your loved one's pilgrim soul—which is to search for the essence of the one you love. Yeats wanted the love of his life to remember when she was "old and grey and full of sleep/ And nodding by the fire..."[94] that, in contrast to the many who had recognized only her surface charms—"who [had] loved [her] beauty with love false or true"—that he had seen "the pilgrim soul in her", *the* searching, yearning soul, her uniqueness and her depth. He knew the genie in her that made her want to leap with joy.

This quality of listening creates two things. First, it creates a power that breaks through hard crusts, what Professor Needleman calls "crusts of worldliness." He says, "it is a worldly crust that snuffs out the light of the self. A hard, worldly crust stultifies your life and prevents your inner being from growing."[95]

The hard work of listening has to do with breaking through each other's worldly crusts so that the Light of the soul can shine through. By listening to each other's pilgrim souls, each other's worldly crusts are dislodged, and your spirits are sent soaring. Together you rise toward the transcendent reference point at the heart of reality that gives life meaning. You ascend together toward the eternal realm of truth, beauty, and goodness.

A love worth its salt inspires a shared yearning for that infinite realm, and a great love—a true love—takes you into that dimension.

When Soul Appears

The second result of the shared search for each other's pilgrim souls is the growing ability to distinguish between the real and the unreal, between temporal values and spiritual ones.

What Baucus and Philemon did for each other was to heighten each other's discriminating powers, so that when the gods Jupiter and Mercury came to visit their village, Baucus and Philemon recognized them and received them with open hearts and embracing arms. The quality of their long-term love had enabled them to recognize the presence of the Divine—a contrast to the rest of the outwardly-turned and inwardly-impoverished villagers who failed to recognize the gods and blindly turned them away.

And now, the rest of the story …

Listen!

> Having received the gods, Jupiter and Mercury, in their tiny cottage, Baucus and Philemon were asked to leave their poor house to climb a steep mountain, guided by the gods. The two old people both did as they were told and, leaning on their sticks, struggled up the long slope. From their vantage point, at the top of the mountain they looked down to see. They noticed that in the town everything had become desolate. No buildings any longer existed but one! The only structure remaining was their house, where they had lived, truly serving each other. They then watched astonished as their poor hut was transformed into a temple of the gods. Marble columns took the place of wooden support, the thatch grew yellow, till the roof seemed to be made of gold.

> The door appeared magnificently adorned with carvings and marble paving the earthen floor.[96]

The message is that this couple's long, slow, unnoticed work of active listening, of being attuned to the highest in each other, had created an enduring love resulting in total transfiguration.

Chapter Fourteen: Intelligence

I WAS SIXTEEN when three songs in a row on FM radio totally captivated me. They were the first three songs on the flip side of the Moody Blues album: *To Our Children's Children's Children*.

I was on fire in response—my deepest longings ignited. It was in some sense a religious experience, more real and vital to me than anything.

Nothing has changed. Years later, if I listen to "Gypsy," "Eternity Road," and "Candle of Life," I am transported into a transcendental realm of beauty and meaning. A taste for the infinite was awakened then. A deep desire for eternity. It was a taste and feel for a level of spiritual experience that went far beyond anything I'd been exposed to at my local church … or anywhere else, for that matter.

Years later at the Master Yoga Academy in La Jolla, California, a teacher described human beings as possessing an innate yearning for transcendence. This reinforced my deepening sense that we were born for transcendence, built for something more than the here and now. My conviction was being confirmed that this world is not all there is. Another world forever calls to us.

That experience as a teenager was an awakening to intelligence, or *higher mind*. When this quality of mind is awakened, according to the Irish poet/

philosopher, John O'Donohue, "the search begins, and you can never go back. From then on, you are inflamed with a special longing that will never again let you linger in the lowlands of complacency and partial fulfillment."[97]

This depth of intelligence is an upsurge of spiritual desire. It's a flashing forth of spiritual energy. An almost irresistible energy wells up from deep within, and you're in a region or realm of intelligence that goes well beyond being merely clever or smart.

It was George Orwell who envisioned in his book *1984* what a society would look like that had dispensed with this calibre of intelligence. Orwell foresaw a society of smoothed-out human beings, now robotic members of a collectivistic herd. All were politically and social correct and collectively ignorant of higher realms of intelligence.

Someone who climbed into the heights and depths of this true intelligence was the Sufi Master Martin Lings, a former student of C.S. Lewis. He recalls when he received the greatest inspiration of his life upon hearing Lewis on the medieval understanding of the human soul and its faculties:

> I can see him now and hear him now. Lewis described the faculties of the soul as arranged in a hierarchy. The highest faculty of the soul is called *intellectus* in Latin, which can be translated as 'intellectual intuition.' [the immediate awareness of the eternal.] *Intellectus* is not for things of this world. This was for me like a flash of lightning for I had never heard of the intellect in its true meaning. It was something wonderful and, in a sense, I never recovered.[98]

In his own inimitable way, John O'Donohue describes this spiritual breakthrough as

When Soul Appears

> To hear the voice of your own soul. It is always there and the more deeply you learn to listen, the greater surprises and discoveries that will unfold. To enter the gentleness of your own soul changes the tone and quality of your life. Your life is no longer consumed by hunger for the next event, experience or achievement. You learn to come down from the treadmill and walk on the earth. You give a new respect for yourself and others and you learn to see how wonderfully precious this one life is. You begin to see through the enchanting veils of illusion that you had taken for reality. You no longer deplete your essence. You know now that your true source is not outside you. Your soul is your true source, and a new energy and passion awakens in you.[99]

This acquisition of intelligence—this sense of the eternal—says O'Donohue, "makes you urgent. You are loath to let compromise, or the threat of danger hold you back from striving toward the summit of fulfillment."[100]

You are never the same again.

Chapter Fifteen: Empty Highs

"EVERYONE WANTS TO be high" says the meditation master, Gurumayi:

> Everyone is high on something or other. Some people are high on their pride, some on their arrogance, some upon their wealth, others on their powers. Still others are high on their clothes, others on the splendor of their impressive homes. Some people are high on their boredom, on their depression, others on their happiness, and still others on their ignorance.[101]

Add to the list of these empty highs another kind of high. It's the high of thinking that you know how God is supposed to be working in the world.

I tend to cringe a little, and sometimes a lot, when I get the impression that somebody has got God—or should I say, his idea of God—all figured out by failing to take seriously the verse in John's Gospel that compares the Spirit of God to the wind: "The wind blows where it wishes, and you hear its sound, but you do not know where it comes from or where it is going."[102]

God's nature, in a phrase, is wind-like, which means that God is not predictable or manageable. "Your God is too small," wrote *New Testament* translator, J.B. Philips, about certain God-constricting theologies. It is this made-up small god who is popular and pursued.

The crowds tend to chase after their small god, full of superstitious zeal, like the crowds who often pressed in on Jesus Christ. Jesus knew that the crowds were looking for *bread only*, that is, for thrills, wonders, and miracles, and not for what He called "the bread of life," the truth that would endure when all lesser things had passed away.

If you've got a god too small on your brain, inevitably there will be a crisis when your idea is put to the test. Gurumayi describes a situation in which a man gave her a letter in which he cursed God because his wife was dying of cancer. He was angry that his "God of mercy" wasn't intervening to save her. He had clogged his brain with ideas about what God was supposed to be and do, though he claimed not to believe in God.

Cynically, he told Gurumayi about how people come up with their ideas about God:

> A child wants to look up to someone and the child thinks his parents are perfect and makes them his deities. As he grows up, he is always searching for some hidden, higher power to replace them, until he says, 'the unseen force is God. Everyone wants something superior, so we create something unseen and unknown—the idea of God.'[103]

In this man's estimation, religion is all make-believe. It's an illusion and has no future. Yet he felt let down by the God he didn't believe in!

When Soul Appears

Gurumayi's response, wisely, was not to argue. Instead, she invited the man to keep coming to the chanting and meditation sessions: "Why don't you keep coming? Why don't you taste and see for a while and see how it goes? Let's see what transpires."[104] She then gave him a rose to take to his dying wife.

As the man visited his wife, she noticed something different about her husband. He was changing somehow. He wasn't aware of it, but she saw it. Thus, as she was dying, she became happier and happier because of her changed husband, a husband who was engaged in spiritual practices.

One day, the man reported back to Gurumayi: "I don't know what happened. I didn't believe in God, but now I do."[105]

Gurumayi observed that the man's experience had become "solid, absolutely concrete." He was experiencing a liberation. How had this come about? "Through meditation he had become free from his fixed ideas."[106] She explains:

> It isn't that God is an idea: It is that you have the idea that God is an idea. Therefore, when you liberate yourself from that idea, you experience peace. The man liberated himself from the idea that the God in whom he didn't believe was taking his wife away from him. When he separated himself from this concept, he experienced peace. Later he was able to give that peace and love to his children, and they were able to cope with their mother's death, with separation, because their father had experienced an internal separation from his own fixed ideas. Because of this inner separation from his idea of God, he experienced union with God, union with Divinity. We arrive at the experience of God as

> we free ourselves from our ideas, our concepts, our beliefs. Then we recognize the God within ourselves and the God within others.[107]

It was a shift of awareness from a God-constricting construction of the mind to a higher experience of the energy of the soul. This shift involves the recognition of the Divine that lies hidden in the depths of one's own soul. As Jesus said: "The kingdom of God cometh not with observation: neither shall they say, Lo, here! Or, lo there! For, behold, the kingdom of God is within you."[108]

None of these highs is worth anything; hence my question—so high, so what?

A high in contrast that is worth something is that blessed high that occurs when the mind calms and becomes profoundly still. Such a mind is letting go of its fancies and claims. It is disarming itself of limiting ideas and concepts by relaxing into the soul.

This was my experience one night when I heard in a dream the voice of one of my sons when he was maybe four or five years old. It was his little boy voice, a voice I hadn't heard for almost thirty years. It was unmistakably his voice and no other. I heard him clearly, full of life and animation. It was his distinctive way of speaking when he was especially thrilled about something. So innocent and so full of wonder. It was as clear a sound as I've ever heard, though I don't recall the content. The voice itself was enough. I woke up feeling utterly astonished. Completely awestruck.

How can I convey how I felt upon entering this timeless zone—this eternal realm, this other world? I was in a dimension beyond space and time. I cannot explain this well enough. Words fail. But the dream had more punch to it and was more vivid, real, and true than anything that happens during daylight hours. This affirms that the best things, the things that the mind can barely comprehend, if at all, are the stuff of life and make life worth living.

When Soul Appears

Wittgenstein, in his *Philosophical Investigations*, describes just how difficult it is to describe the aroma of coffee: "Why can't it be done? Do we lack the words? Have you tried to describe the aroma of coffee and not succeeded?"[109] We flounder and fail to describe the aroma of coffee, just as we stammer to describe a particular dream. Yet our experiences are real. It's just that words are insufficient.

I am thus affirming that there is another realm or dimension beyond this one, a reality of wonder and mystery that sometimes opens as we respond to great literature, music, art, spiritual practices, or, as in my experience, an incredible dream.

The philosopher Daniel Robinson, author of *The Great Ideas of Philosophy* for The Great Courses, speaks to me when he says somewhere that there is a dream world closer to reality than the mere and shifting items seen under the sobering light of day.

Robinson is referencing a realm of mystery and wonder—the real thing—that goes way beyond what can ever be scientifically observed and recorded.

The experience is everything and to be treasured always.

Chapter Sixteen:
A Feeling Beyond Feeling

I'M NOT A joiner. I don't blend in easily, nor do I want to. I'd rather be alone in a corner somewhere, Bose noise cancelling headphones on, listening to Calm Radio. I'm trusting that in heaven there will be corners for introverts, away from the hand-holding crowds singing "Hallelujah."

All my life it's been this way—searching in corners for a certain height and depth of awareness not ordinarily experienced.

Perhaps your quest as well?

A while back, I felt rather out of sorts. To deal with it, I contacted an old friend. I sought the companionship of the poet and playwright Rabindranath Tagore, the first East Indian to win the Nobel Prize for Literature in 1913. To reassemble myself, I watched a documentary about his life of holiness and integrity. In no time flat, I was realigned. I turned to Tagore because I knew that his great mind had expanded into its fullest capacities through mystical dimensions of experience.

Ludwig Wittgenstein, perhaps the twentieth century's greatest philosopher, in like manner, yearned for transcendental realms of experience and thus turned to Tagore for inspiration. As a fan of Tagore, he distinguished himself from the Logical Positivists whose anti-metaphysical stance was that you can only make positive affirmations about what is observed by and through the senses. Resisting the materialistic Positivists, Wittgenstein once literally turned his back on them at a philosophy meeting and proceeded to read aloud from Tagore's writings! He had no respect for the severely shackled mindsets of the Positivists, so he turned his back on them to make the statement that a crucial, essential element was missing in their thinking.

What was missing was a certain essential feeling. It's no ordinary feeling. But, in a sense, *a feeling beyond feeling.*

A feeling beyond emotion.

A certain refined level of feeling.

This deep essential feeling beyond feeling is an instrument of knowledge and as such, indispensable. Indeed, you know squat without it.

Father Anthony Bloom, an Eastern Orthodox priest, claimed that it is crucial to find this deeper level of feeling within yourself in order to encourage spiritual transformation.

To facilitate the awareness of this vital dimension, Bloom gave specific instructions:

> Settle down in your room at a moment when you have nothing else to do. And say, 'I am not with myself,' and 'just be with yourself.' After an amazingly short time, you will most likely feel bored, which teaches us one very useful thing. It gives us insight into the fact that if after ten minutes of being alone with yourself that you feel like that, it is no wonder that others should feel equally bored! Why

> is this so? We have so little to offer our own selves as food for thought, for emotion and for life. If you watch your life carefully, you'll soon discover that we hardly ever live from within outwards. Instead, we respond to incitement and excitement. In other words, we live by reaction. We are completely empty. We don't act from within ourselves but accept a life that is fed from the outside. We are used to things happening that compel us to do other things. How seldom can we live simply by means of the depth and the richness we assume is there within ourselves.[110]

Fr Bloom says that our tendency is to "to live by reaction," which happens because "we are completely empty." We become aware of our own inner vacuity when the attempt is made to be quiet and still. But that is not the end of the story. For it is possible to move through the hollowness into regions of inner depth and richness. The challenge is to remain still long enough for the shift to occur from emptiness to fullness. That fullness is, as I'm describing it, a feeling beyond feeling, a feeling beyond emotion. That level of feeling is a sense of the Divine presence.

Jacob Needleman says that we are born with the capacity for this level of refined feeling but are too often held back by our minds that, in their natural state, are atheistic. In other words, the unregenerate mind is unbelieving. By the atheist mind, Needleman means the isolated intellect of the Logical Positivists for whom refined feeling—feeing beyond feeling—is unknown.

For Fr Anthony Bloom, this sense of a feeling beyond feeling is an experience of the eternal dimension and a pointer to what's to come beyond death. It's the foretaste of a full-scale actualization in the life to come. In this regard, Bloom refers to a verse from the book of Revelation: "To him who overcomes, I will give a white stone, and, on the stone, a new name written."[111]

To him, in other words, who has persevered on the spiritual journey, there will be a revelation in the form of a gift—a white stone with a new name on it.

What new name is that?

It's your ultimate name. The name that will unlock you in the presence of God.

Bloom explains: "Scripture tells us that in the Kingdom of God each of us will receive a white stone with a name written on it, a name known only to God and to the one who receives it."[112] The new name on the stone represents

> the unique relationship that exists between every person and his God, a relationship which is too deep for any other being to perceive or to understand, a depth in us so deep, so great, that none but God can plumb it. That new name is the key to our very being, the key to what we are, the root and cornerstone of our being.

All our lives, says Bloom, we have been moving toward a climactic revelation, which will be the discovery of a deeper identity than we ever knew while alive. It will be "a perfect and unique fulfillment by the God who loves us."[113]

Your destiny then, in these terms, is not to be either blotted out, or lost in the cosmic soup, but rather to be made more fully differentiated than you could ever have dreamed!

Peter Kreeft, the American philosopher, affirms Fr Anthony Bloom: "All of our lives we have been struggling to overcome and to cast off what is false in us as we search for our unique selves — our true selves." There is, according to Kreeft, "a knowledge and destiny that awaits us."[114]

When Soul Appears

Our fullest identity is waiting for us. It is a level of fulfillment beyond our wildest imaginings, when in the presence of the God who loves and recognizes us, we come fully into our own.

I've been describing a journey that begins with the recognition of a certain feeling beyond emotion—a feeling beyond feeling—a sense of the Divine within. The sense of that feeling beyond feeling leads finally to an incomparable glory in the presence of God.

A prayer:

> Give me a candle of the Spirit, O God, as I go down into the deeps of my being. Show me the hidden things, the creatures of my dreams, the storehouse of forgotten memories and hurts. Take me down to the spring of life and tell me my nature and my name. Give me freedom to grow, so that I may become that self, the seed of which You planted in me at my making.[115]

Chapter Seventeen: Dreamers

IN THE EARLY 1930s, a boat carrying 107 mostly British communists arrived in St Petersburg. These were starry-eyed immigrants determined to unite with the (said to be) glorious Soviet Union. They were expecting to arrive in promised land. With one accord, they had believed the false, though glowing, reports—the fake news—that a utopia was about to be realized. It was, so they thought, the dawning of a new age. Heaven on earth was being created by the (reputed to be) fatherly Joseph Stalin.

Well-equipped for the adventure, the 107 arrived "with mountains of trunks, bicycles, and gramophones."[116] These dreamers had "no sense of the tragi-comedy in which they had landed themselves." For "in a matter of days, they had been swindled out of their money and stripped of their possessions and had to be looked after by sympathetic Westerners."[117]

And yet these dreamers were not alone.

So many others, led by the likes of the Irish/British playwright George Bernard Shaw, were similarly blinded by Soviet propaganda and their allies, many Western reporters. Many have noted: "The brute facts about the Soviet Union were always available, but many people found many reasons to deceive themselves and others about its true nature."[118]

Among the dreamers (back in Britain) was an Anglican priest, Hewlett Johnson, who became the dean (not the archbishop) of Canterbury in 1931. For thirty-three years thereafter, this priest, who came to be called the Red Dean of Canterbury, devoted himself to arguing that Soviet Communism was heaven on earth. Cheerleading for Stalin, he exclaimed: "While we're waiting for God, Russia is doing it!"[119]

During the time Stalin was engaged in mass murder, the dean wrote in *The Socialist Sixth of the World* that "nothing strikes the visitor to the Soviet Union more forcibly than the complete absence of fear."[120]

About his persistent blindness, it was said that "no Communist outrage could put Johnson off his stride."[121] Indeed, Johnson praised the Soviets for their toleration of religion, and upon meeting Stalin, reported excitedly that the great man favoured freedom of conscience. For his efforts, in 1951 Johnson was awarded The Stalin Peace Prize and then The Order of the Red Banner of Labour.

But it wasn't just Stalin before whom the priest swooned. When he met Chairman Mao, the Chinese dictator, he again felt enraptured, describing the "great" man as having a countenance that was all "lit up with warmth and radiance." Why, Mao had even said goodbye to him, the Red Dean reported, "lingering in the courtyard to point out a lovely flowering tree."[122]

The Red Dean was a great friend to Stalin and Mao, but deplorably an enemy of Victor Kravchenko, author of the book *I Chose Freedom* (1949). If ever a voice should have been heeded in exposing the Soviet Union for the great evil that it was, it was Kravchenko's, who had every credential to make him believable. Kravchenko was not only from the Soviet Union but also from a working-class background. He had been educated there as an engineer and had become a party activist. He'd also held a prominent position as an industrial administrator.

When Soul Appears

But in response to his book about freedom from Soviet tyranny, he faced a huge backlash from the Soviets and their Western supporters. Eventually, Kravchenko launched a lawsuit against a French publication that had claimed his book was full of lies and a collaborative effort with the United States.

The trial lasted for two months and received a lot of publicity. Well-known writers attended, including Albert Camus, Arthur Koestler, Jean-Paul Sartre, and Simone de Beauvoir. On Kravchenko's side were refugees like himself and former prisoners of the Soviet concentration camps. Against him were the Soviets and Hewlett Johnson, the Red Dean of Canterbury!

These together testified to the wonders of the Soviet system and discredited and denounced Kravchenko. On display was a clash between truth tellers and liars.

Concerning the lying supporters of the U.S.S.R., Arthur Koestler, known best for his book *Darkness at Noon*, wrote about how to account for "the operations of the deluded mind."[123] The deluded mind, he said, engages in "elaborate maneuverings to defend its own citadel of faith against the hostile incursions of doubt."[124] He himself had once done this, fully immersed in "a blinkered, sectarian outlook on the world."[125] But upon travelling widely in the Soviet Union (1932–33), he saw the effects of the Great Famine caused by Stalin's forced collectivization of the land: "I saw entire villages deserted, railway stations blocked by crowds of begging families, and the starving infants with stick-like arms, puffed up bellies and cadaverous heads."[126]

Koestler then began to struggle against what he called an "inner censor" that had kept him and many others from the truth. That inner censor was an ideological shutter over the soul that smothered the soul's innate ability to perceive what is true. Such an inner censor is so powerful, says Koestler, that it serves to be "more reliable and effective than any official censorship."[127] He describes that inner censor as an "automatic sorting machine" that suppresses truth in favour of lies."[128] Everyone he knew was gripped by the inner censor, and all were therefore experts at self-deception. No external Iron Curtain was needed for those whose own private iron curtains did the job of "protecting their illusions against the intrusions of reality."[129]

The only escape from the gripping power of the inner censor, according to Koestler, was to allow yourself to struggle with the gap between your beliefs (your delusions) and reality—to the point of being inwardly torn apart by the cognitive dissonance. An enormous struggle is required to awaken the seeker after truth to a completely different frame of mind, a truly liberated mind. To break the iron grip of the inner censor, the truth seeker must grant to himself, "The possibility of doubting. The possibility of making a mistake. The possibility of searching and experimenting. The possibility of saying 'no' to any authority, literary, artistic, philosophic, religious, social, and even political."[130] To unclamp yourself from the vice of the inner censor you must tackle it head on by developing a skeptical, critical spirit. Then finally, that inner censor can be put out of commission, replaced by a "counter-revolutionary mind."[131]

The American philosopher, Daniel N. Robinson, says the same about the necessity of the critical spirit:

> You must be able to say that no matter how much this means to me, no matter how centered my being is on this pattern of beliefs, no matter how close I am personally and emotionally, and even romantically, to those who hold such convictions, I must reserve the right to question and to doubt. No position, therefore, especially your own, is beyond criticism. In fact, you must always be prepared fully to launch a skeptical spotlight upon even your most cherished beliefs, opinions and values. I will retain this skeptical bias as an obligation owed to my own rationality, my own integrity. If you lose that reason and suspend that criticality,

become gullible, and accept anything that custom serves up, you enter the life of a puppet on a string, the life of a slave.[132]

If we fail to cultivate this questioning, critical spirit, we risk falling into that state of dreaminess that in every generation appears to be ever so willing to swallow the latest lies and deceptions of its own day and time.

Chapter Eighteen: Full of It?

HIPPIAS, A CHARACTER in Plato's writings, is described in Robert E. Cushman's book *Therapeia* as someone who was full of knowledge about inconsequential things, a sort of ancient Trivial Pursuit expert. He was thus regarded by Plato as a sophist, that is, a pseudo-philosopher.

This is to be something of a poser who perhaps looks good on some level to many, but to the wise and discerning, is closer to a charlatan.

Was he like the sort of gas bag still knocking about today who talks your ear off with superficialities while somehow oblivious to first things—essential things—things that truly matter? Plato seems to think this about Hippias, that he was someone full of the superfluous, the sort of mentality that is chock-full of sophistry.

From a Platonic perspective, the sophistry of Hippias is the chief characteristic of the worldly man who is only a success strategist or success monger, and who therefore is a man sorely lacking—an empty suit, though dressed in a finely tailored one, and singularly unqualified to be a true teacher of knowledge and wisdom.

For Plato, Hippias is the impoverished man. He is the ignorant man whose worldly attainments are regarded as nothing compared to someone who has attained spiritual wisdom. Plato had only disdain for those whose habit of mind and way of life was a focus on the acquisition of knowledge about many things while skipping past the search for essential, or higher, things.

Hence the Platonic perspective is that "wisdom is remote from the mental state of one who is surfeited with knowledge of many things, [for whom] the knowledge which encumbers his mind is incredibly numerous, …the content [being] fifty-seven varieties of odds and ends. [Put another way:] No matter how encyclopedic a man's mind, or how learned he may be in the sciences, he is not therefore equipped to give good counsel."[133]

For Plato, the ability to give good counsel comes only from that one who is "a lover of truth and wisdom, from that person who strives after true being."[134]

Plato's critique of Hippias is that he is crammed full of a lot of specialized, external knowledge, but is inside an empty sop. He is skilled at skimming along on the surface of things—perhaps smooth, slick, and clever—but ultimately a vacuous, empty messenger, in a phrase, brimful of nothing, which means to possess nothing of real substance or value.

In contrast to Hippias, a specialist in the superficial, is another kind of person who, through her way of life—her art, teaching and friendships—has the effect of inspiring a desire for a deeper life, a spiritual one. She's the kind of person who catapults you out of yourself into new and greater dimensions of being. She's the antithesis of a Hippias, a friend whose quality-of-life points to transcendence, who stirs in you a longing to cultivate a daily prayer and meditation practice. Her sanctifying effect is that you are seized with a longing to know God.

In Platonic terms, upon meeting someone like this, you aspire to recollect yourself as you begin to recognize and care about your own spiritual nature. You then begin to make efforts to bring yourself together fully, to gather yourself through the splendour of the recognition that you are more than a material man or woman. You understand that you aren't just a body or just a mind but, more deeply, a soul, with Spirit shining through.

You understand and recognize, as in Wordsworth's poem, that you've come into the world not as a blank slate but with an enormous spiritual capacity:

> Our birth is but a sleep and a forgetting;
>
> The soul that rises with us, our life's star,
>
> Hath had elsewhere its setting
>
> And cometh from afar;
>
> Not in entire forgetfulness,
>
> And not in utter nakedness,
>
> But trailing clouds of glory do we come
>
> From God, who is our home:
>
> Heaven lies about us in our infancy![135]

You understand that the Light of God is shining through the newborn child. Seeing her through a spiritual lens, you understand that the child is not some little, soulless thing and as such, some sort of fluke of the universe. No. Her birth is an affirmation that there is meaning and purpose in the universe.

But as the story goes in every generation, with growth comes a downward spiral into spiritual forgetfulness, often solidified in late adolescence as the "shades of the prison-house (peer pressure & such) begin to close upon the growing girl or boy."[136]

Alas, the teenager loses touch with her capacity for wonder and joy. The heart closes and she becomes preoccupied with perhaps becoming a modern-day Hippias, going after success after success while ignoring higher things.

And then that teenager becomes a woman who continues to make it her practice and habit to forget that her roots are in the Divine, and who gets caught up in imagining that she's the kingpin of her own existence. The hope remains, however, that either a crisis or an awakening of spiritual longing will move the young adult toward the task of recognition and recollection as she seeks to bring herself together in a response to the Divine Light.

Not long ago, I was invited to a cocktail party. Cringe …

The evening began with a non-conversation but then, thankfully, a real one followed! During the first non-conversation, two bodies stood in front of me who, as far as I could tell, were there but not there, if you know what I mean.

These two were present, but absent.

Their presence was an absence.

I couldn't find any way to connect with either of them. If the evening had gone on like that, I would have gone home concluding that I been to a non-event, to another empty cocktail party where nothing meant anything—an entirely unmemorable event.

But then, from out of nowhere as it seemed, an elderly gentleman approached me in a friendly manner. I was astonished by his immediate interest and vital presence. But no sooner had he made his presence felt before someone bolted between us in a burst of joviality, which in effect interrupted a conversation barely begun.

When Soul Appears

Not wishing to just stand there passively, I politely eased myself away, saying gently to the older gentleman, "There's no social obligation. Don't worry."

I expected that to be the end of it. But a while later, to my surprise, the man approached me a second time. Was he a nut, I wondered, or something more? The engagement between us was instantaneous on so many levels, yet on one level, he was way beyond me, for he was a retired professor of mathematics, and I can barely add.

It quickly became plain that we shared a search for depth and meaning, so we began to engage together in the magic of inquiry. In our own way, we turned the cocktail party into one of Plato's Symposiums, at least in our corner of the room. There was between us absolutely no surface talk at all.

His wife, upon noticing the connection commented, as her eyes sparkled, "He needs this kind of interaction." It was evident how much she loved and supported him.

Do you know what stood out most about the math professor? It wasn't so much his considerable knowledge about this or that, but that somehow, he was animated by streams of living water flowing from within. He was that striking presence and saved my evening from meaninglessness.

My new friend was, in other words, not at all like the ancient character Hippias, the sophist, the success-monger, described by Robert Cushman as "stuffed with scientific and historical information—ever ready and willing to disgorge his learning in the presence of any group of open-mouthed bystanders."[137]

No. The professor was in no way a fake or poser. He was the opposite—a true philosopher, a humble lover of wisdom. I would describe my new friend as someone whose way of being and thinking arose from an awakened essence. Unlike Hippias or his modern counterparts, the professor was someone whose life had broken out of what Huston Smith calls our "cabined condition." The professor knew that level of soul that Smith describes as "situated behind the senses," which "sees through the eyes without being seen and hears with the ears without being heard—which lies there deeper than the mind."[138]

My new friend was well acquainted with that life-giving dimension. It informed and inspired his life and manner. I felt blessed at the cocktail party not to have met a sophist, like Hippias—*full of it,* but an inspired man "full of Spirit." Thus inspired, I had a great time at the cocktail party!

I went home full and slept well.

Chapter Nineteen: Seduced by Relativism

A FRIEND OF mine grew up in Communist Poland. As a boy, aware that he could expect only lies from his country's radio waves, he used to spend many hours secretly listening to foreign shortwave radio broadcasts to learn the truth. He says that listening in this way, while living in the pressure cooker of a communist tyranny, had the effect of sharpening his powers of discernment and increasing his sensitivity to all matters of good and evil.

The truth, he learned early on, was something that had to be searched for. Comforting lies, in contrast, were readily available. Nevertheless, despite the moral clarity he had acquired as a child, he found that years later, after moving first to Great Britain and then to Canada, he began to lose his moral ground. Intellectually inclined, he recalls that he began to lose his bearings in response to the charm and seductive power of the impressive writings of certain leftist British and Canadian publications.

Entranced by what he called "certain well-written articles," he failed for a time to discern the spirit of relativism (the notion that no absolute values exist) that seeped through the pages. He states that the effect of being absorbed in this way was that his powers of discernment began to blur and slacken. He was, as he eventually came to see, being "seduced by relativism."

His ever-watchful father diagnosed his condition and warned that his son's soul was being smothered out of existence. My friend's father cautioned him against the spirit or attitude of relativism, which is that pernicious mindset or orientation that asserts that when it comes to making moral judgements, there are no Divine imperatives or absolutes.

There are, in contrast, always and only relative choices, reflecting the notion that one thing is as good as another, or that somehow everything is beautiful in its own way.

In other words, there is no such thing as the truth, only *my truth*, or *your truth*. This, of course, is a great lie, for some things are anything but beautiful. Some things are by nature false and ugly and need to be discerned and exposed as such. For example, it's a starry-eyed foolishness to regard a totalitarian government as in any sense beautiful. Totalitarianism is rather a horror. A clear-eyed person with an intact soul understands this. Such a seer sees through what is dressed up to look good. Thus, a tyranny is always ugly, which my friend knew from firsthand experience of Communist Poland.

This was similarly discerned by the Lutheran pastor, Dietrich Bonhoeffer, who in the early days of Hitler's rise to power in Germany knew the man to be a looming tyrant. Undeceived, Bonhoeffer saw that Hitler was a depraved human being who embodied absolute evil. Such a man, Bonhoeffer clearly understood, would never respond either to reason or appeasement. Thus, while many were mesmerized by Hitler's oratory, Bonhoeffer stood firm in opposition.

Now, the spirit of relativism might also be called the spirit of the age. Its nature is a subjectivist spirit (the only thing that matters is what *I*, the subject, happen to feel or prefer without regard for objective standards and values) and is especially dominant and prevalent in today's landscape. It is highly likely that in the coffee shop where I write, most everyone around me is a relativist and would tend not to speak of absolute, objective values that require an adequate response from us, but rather assume that all judgements concerning values are matters only of one's own personal taste or preference.

My friend's father challenged him to listen to other voices to bring him back to his soul. A good son, he listened and vowed that he would search for the practical wisdom of dissenting voices.

Today, many years later, my friend is known as someone of high moral principles and great integrity. He had not fully realized during his early days in Britain and in Canada that it was not only in Communist Poland that a seeker of truth would have to make an extra effort to listen to distant, truth-bearing voices. As C.S. Lewis warned, back in the 1940s—the poison of subjectivism had spread to Great Britain. It was rearing its ugly head in British classrooms.

In *The Abolition of Man*, Lewis made the case that this poisonous subjectivism, the relativistic spirit, was creeping into children's classrooms through their textbooks. Now, seventy years later, the poison Lewis warned about is everywhere. So, for example, if you happen to be at a Vancouver dinner party and dare even casually to suggest a different point of view on some issue that the spirit of our age has declared already settled, you can almost guarantee that you will hear an angry voice, or several, scream back at you: "Well, that's just your opinion!" This will be followed by the statement that: "You're intolerant and judgemental!"

You will, in other words, be shouted down by the people who run around saying that everything is beautiful in its own way. Everything is beautiful, say the relativists, except that they will never accept as beautiful the moral absolutes of the world's great religions. Instead, the ideals and standards of the world's great religions are on their hit list.

How often have I seen the so-called lovers of tolerance and diversity—the everything is beautiful crowd—turn suddenly into a swarming, shouting mob. They are against moral absolutes but strikingly absolutist when it comes to their own judgements.

Professor Jean Elshtain tells of when she interviewed a candidate for a political science job at her school. For the interviewee, everything was only a subjectivist preference, so Dr Elshtain challenged him: "It is a curious thing, is it not? When Martin Luther King delivered his great speech, he cried, 'I have a dream!' not, 'I have a preference!' How do you explain this? Is there a difference?"[139]

The interviewee was flustered and would not bring himself to acknowledge that there is any difference between an absolute, commanding moral imperative and some milquetoast preference. He saw no difference because he'd spent years suppressing his own highest and best instincts. In other words, he'd been drinking, like so many others, the poison of his own subjectivity.

C.S. Lewis warned that in the reduction of values to feelings "something precious and irreparable is being lost."[140]

Indeed.

Chapter Twenty:
A Vague but Vital Intuition

"MAN IS NOT fulfilled," writes Raimon Panikkar, the philosopher who wrote *The Rhythm of Being*, "solely by what we perceive through the senses, comprehend with the mind, or feel with the heart." More than these modes of apprehension—senses, mind and heart— "we also have," says Panikkar, "an intuition, albeit vague, that there is something more beyond what can be touched, known or felt."[141]

This intuition, however faint, nudges you toward a greater possibility of fulfillment than what is possible in terms of this world only. Something in you—an inner voice of some kind—prompts your attention toward a level of experience beyond what the senses, mind and heart can grasp. What's inwardly stirring, say the great sages and seers, is a certain inner capacity that all possess but many ignore. The great visionaries urge us to listen to this quiet inner force. If we do, the quality and course of our lives will be forever altered. Upon heeding this special call, our perceptive powers are lit up, and what is called *third eye seeing* comes into play. Our own spiritual centre opens to unleash a power that will tie together, or integrate every part of us, resulting in the experience of the fullness of life. If it's true, the human being's possibility of fulfillment is directly related to the degree that he becomes aware of and follows what may feel at first to be only a dim intuition beyond the physical senses leading into that deeper realm that unites the others. Our possibility of fulfillment, or a sense of completion, depends on it.

But our culture typically prizes the kind of seeing done with the mind, senses and heart only. It's a deficient focus and indicative of an impoverished condition, because it leaves out the essential, spiritual dimension. According to the spiritually-realized adept, to live like that, which is not to live very well, is to live in a constricted, bound and blind condition. This is the natural, carnal, or unregenerate state. By its nature, this level of existence is unbelieving or atheistic.

When your energies are given over to this natural state, third-eye seeing is suppressed or covered over. If acknowledged at all, it tends to be either downplayed or underestimated. The most important thing about you—your inner capacity for spiritual realization—is treated as something inconsequential.

How easy it is to miss the adventure into deeper levels of awareness and possibilities of fulfillment. In fact, our entire society is structured to ensure that such an adventure will never even begin. We live in a world and a culture that suffocates the still, small voice, the vague intuition, by a preoccupation with external events and happenings—thrills and spills, bread and circuses. A Roman writer described the state of the Roman population in its sorry decline: "Two things only, the people anxiously desire—bread and circuses."[142]

To keep the Roman populace pacified, the government distributed free food and staged huge spectacles. The officials created their own versions of the Super Bowl—great extravaganzas to ensure that most everyone was permanently doped. It's like Orwell's *1984*, where the mass of the population sits in the public houses, perpetually stupefied by the steady flow of cheap beer—their souls numbed by the constant sensory bombardment of loud music and news reports coming at them through huge video screens. If there are lots of new sensations, most are not inclined to question their imprisonment.

But we can break out of these soul-limiting prisons to turn life into an adventure of never-ending possibilities of illumination. The way is to listen hard for the barely perceptible intuition—to that still small voice or whisper that sometimes wakes you up at night. If you do, it has the potential to be the single greatest factor in determining the direction and calibre of your life.

This is exactly how Stephen Buhner's spiritual adventure began when he directed his attention to his own intuitive sense: "My recognition of this feeling sense (this vague intuition), I regard as the most important insight of my life."[143] For Buhner, to follow this inner sense was to go down the road less travelled. It meant acting against everything he'd been taught. Those around him, friends and relatives, would not let him go easily. They pushed back against his concern to heed this inner sense. "I was to find," he says, that "no other quality of my character was more intensely assaulted."[144] The tactic used against him was that someone would try to "analytically overwhelm me with mental commentary and data."[145] When young, he says, "I was too unsophisticated to respond in any meaningful sense."[146] Later he learned how to manage the assaults and realized that he was the one with clarity. His abusive, wordy attackers were the confused ones. As the scientist-turned-philosopher Michael Polanyi put it, he had "tacit knowing: *he knew more than he could tell.*" However hard to express, it was the most important dynamic in his life.

As Stephen Buhner and Michael Polanyi learned to trust their own intuitions, so did Borghild Baldauf in 1997 when she was sitting in the "small quiet backroom of my home listening to a monthly radio program on different world religions."[147] One evening she heard about the spiritual experience of Dr. Carla Kumar, who had experienced a spiritual initiation through the Indian scholar-saint, Swami Lakshmanjoo: "There was something in Carla Kumar's experience, her evident sincerity, simplicity, devotion and joy that somehow seemed to fit, or resonate perfectly, with her own searching heart."[148] She then began to realize that a no-holds-barred response was required of her. In time, as she followed this inner call, she found herself on the other side of the world at an Ashram. She describes its atmosphere as having both "peace and intensity,"[149] an indication to her that the place was authentic. There, as she sat listening to "the fervent recitation of ancient hymns," Borghild experienced the music as "seeds, falling on a soil which increasingly was open and ready to receive."[150] On the last day of this enriching time, a strange thing occurred. "I started weeping and for hours there was no end of my tears. Fortunately, I was alone that day because it was as if—for the first time in my life—I had lost control of myself. Completely helpless, I was unable to form a clear idea, lost in the welter of disparate emotions and the vain attempt to get the rudder back into my hands again. There was nothing I could do except to go to the meditation room, prostrate myself there and let go of everything. What had happened? During the night my former life had passed by like in a flash."[151]

It was a homecoming experience for Borghild Baldauf. Her experience was of being spiritually purged, deconstructed and properly put together. It was the greatest experience of her life. What had begun years before as an undefined feeling in response to a radio broadcast had become for Borghild a life-transforming experience. Her own life's greatest possibility occurred because she took an indeterminate, but persistent feeling seriously and followed it, in her case, to the ends of the earth.

She followed that inner sensation—that vague intuition—that Panikkar says "is hidden in the innermost Man like a mysterious root."[152] Upon being stirred, it begins to sizzle to perhaps lead you toward the greatest possibility of your life.

Chapter Twenty-One: Marta

WHAT'S PARTICULAR ABOUT the Christian faith is its emphasis on the personal. Its core affirmation is the view of God as person. The remarkable consequence of this emphasis, according to the sociologist Peter Berger, is that "the personhood of God gives ultimate validity to the personhood of human beings. [This emphasis] emphatically validates the infinite worth and dignity of the human person."[153]

The incomparable Christian perspective is that personality is the glory of the universe, which gives Christianity its "crucially distinctive quality."[154] The person matters. In a phrase, *you as you* matter. This is affirmed in the Eastern Orthodox communion rite when the priest addresses you by name when you receive communion. It is you as a particular you who's being recognized. The Eucharist itself is an affirmation that the highest and deepest point of contact between man and God is a deeply personal event.

It has sometimes been expressed, especially by mystics, that this emphasis upon the personal dimension is an unenlightened level of understanding that must be overcome or transcended. The thinking is that the sense you have of yourself as a distinct somebody must be abrogated. You've got to get past your illusory sense as a separate self. You must let go of your limited identity to realize your identity with God, or the impersonal That. You've got to let go of your sense of yourself in order to enter that deeper reality, a non-personal dimension. You are to break past what the Jewish philosopher Martin Buber called the "I-Thou" relationship. It is thought that access to that higher impersonal realm can only be reached if I leave behind "all vestiges of my empirical self."[155]

This was Meister Eckhart's point, according to Berger, when he distinguished between "God, the personal God of Biblical revelation, and the Godhead, the impersonal divinity of mystical experience."[156] Mystics like Eckhart use the language of a merger with the Divine that, in a sense, takes you out. Thus, it is often said that in the mystical experience that nothing remains of you. In other words, you as you are no more.

In the mystical experience, you have become God, or have realized that you are That. But you are most certainly not you. Game over. I've never thought that those who talk about a mystic fusion with the Divine ever quite pull it off.

The idea of what it means for a person and God to become one must be qualified. Even in the very best of friendships, there is at once a sense of union and of separation. You become one but remain two. And if you become utterly absorbed in someone to the point that you lose your identity in him or her, something (I'm trying to put this mildly) may not be quite right.

For where there is a strong and vital union between persons in a friendship or marriage, personality isn't obliterated. It is rather sharpened and enhanced. You become more yourself than perhaps you've ever been. You become more particular, distinct, and stronger.

I share Peter Berger's question about the nature of ultimate reality. He asks: "I want to know whether this reality is in any way capable of interacting with me in a way that does not negate my own personhood."[157]

Berger's question implies a strong 'yes' to the experience of union with the Divine, but a strong 'no' to the negation of personhood. For Berger, certain experiences have served to clarify his thinking about the meaning of union with God. He tells the story:

> On my first trip to India, I was in Calcutta, on my way to visit a religious scholar, when I encountered a Hindu funeral procession. It is a shocking sight for a modern Westerner, since there is no coffin—the corpse, in this instance an old man, lies exposed on a wooden plank. There was a rather small number of mourners in the procession, and some of them were chanting. They were chanting from *The Bhagavad Gita—The Song of the Lord*, where it reads: 'Even as a person casts off worn-out clothes and puts on others that are new, so the embodied Self casts off worn-out bodies and enters into others that are new. Weapons cut it not; fire burns it not; water wets it not; the wind does not wither it. This Self cannot be cut, nor burnt, nor wetted, nor withered. Eternal, all-pervading, unchanging, immovable, the Self is the same for ever. This Self is said to be unmanifest, incomprehensible, and unchangeable. Therefore, knowing It to be so, you should not grieve.'[158]

This is supposed to be a source of consolation to any mourner, but it's of no comfort to Peter Berger, whose response was: "If I had been one of the mourners in the funeral procession, I would not have been consoled."[159]

Berger then worked out for himself that he could only believe in a religion that upheld three essentials: "the infinite value of this person, this body, and this world."[160]

Since the Gita doesn't emphasize "the unique value of these (three) empirical realities," but tends to regard them as illusions to get over, Berger felt himself compelled to say no to the Gita, but he adds the point that to say no doesn't mean that "the experience underlying the worldview of the Gita is simply an illusion."[161]

No. The Hindus have a point, he says, as do the mystics of the Christian religion, which is that when "the self loses itself in an ocean of universal being it is a real experience." He adds that "it would be presumptuous and implausible to propose that this experience is nothing but several millennia's worth of illusion."[162]

Indeed, Berger celebrates the "liberating quality" of such a mystic experience: "To give up the tensions and contractions of the self is a great emotional relief."[163] And thus, the mystic experience is real but must be better interpreted as an experience of both union and separation at once.

I know from my own experiences of deep meditation that I can sometimes feel that I have entirely lost a sense of self. Yet I emerge, so far anyway, from the stillness with an enhanced sense of my own personhood.

I'm still Al.

This takes me back to a Sunday ten years ago at St Herman's Orthodox Church in Langley, British Columbia, when a baby girl named Marta was placed in my arms by her mother. My new job as Marta's godfather was to present her to the priest for Holy Communion. The event that day happened swiftly and smoothly, which was a relief, as Marta had been giving the impression that she wasn't going to cooperate. I knew how to handle boys, since I had raised three sons, but a little girl?

On that momentous day, I came away with the thought that there's never been another creation like Marta, and never will be. She is a special child of God—entirely unique. Marta has her own shining singularity. I thought,

Surely, the God who created Marta is invested in preserving her, which is indeed the Christian promise and the point of this chapter.

The *person* is the glory of the universe. Therefore, Marta is the glory of the universe. As such, Marta has an eternal destiny as a distinctive being. In Christian terms, Marta's destiny is to be transfigured and glorified.

For that reason, her parents bring their little girl every Sunday to a church sanctuary where the sign at its entrance reads: "Enter the place of Transfiguration."

The sign does not say "Enter the place of Obliteration."

People can choose to obliterate themselves elsewhere.

Every Sunday, I have the privilege of presenting Marta to the priest for Holy Communion. That action, perhaps more than anything else, has enabled me to sort out and clarify what I most deeply believe.

Afterword:

JUST AS THE energy of soul can appear, it can easily disappear. Soul disappears when we are distracted, thereby dissipating that life giving energy. Every day we are either gathering our attention towards soulfulness or dispersing it. Every day, in other words, we are either finding ourselves or losing ourselves.

The challenge upon breaking through into transcendence is to remain in the great mystery. The challenge is to live within that zone of awareness all the time. One way to remain vigilant is to repeat the Jesus prayer: *Lord Jesus Christ, Son of God, have mercy on me*. For myself, I love to repeat: *God is the soul of my soul, the soul of my soul*. It is an affirmation. It is a prayer of the heart and as Jesus said, "Blessed are the pure in heart for they shall see God."[164]

Notes

1. Jacob Needleman, *Lost Christianity*, Doubleday & Company, New York, 1980, 175.
2. Colin Wilson, *The Man and His Mind,* Howard F. Dossor, Long Mead, Great Britain, Element Books Ltd. 1990, 326.
3. Colin Wilson, *The Outsider*, United States: Diversion Books, 2014, 222.
4. Jacob Needleman, *What Is God?* United States: Penguin Publishing Group, 2009, 14.
5. Ibid.
6. Needleman, *What is God?* 14.
7. Jordan Peterson, *Maps of Meaning: The Architecture of Belief*, New York, Routledge, 1999, xvi.
8. Ibid., xvii.
9. Needleman, Ibid.
10. Ibid.
11. Needleman, 3
12. Ibid., 5
13. Needleman, *What is God?* 21–24.
14. Christopher Tompkins, The Dance of Shakti—An Introduction to Goddess Tantra.doc Created Date: 12/11/2008 3:42:02 PM.
15. Rabindranath Tagore, *The Religion of Man*, India: Rupa & Company, 2002, 74.
16. Ibid.
17. Swami Chidvilasananda, *The Yoga of Discipline*, New York, Syda Foundation, 1996, 34.
18. Edith Stein, *The Hidden Life, Essays, Meditations and Spiritual Texts*, ICS Publications, Washington D.C. 1997, 2014, 28.
19. Ibid.
20. Ibid.
21. Ibid.

22. George Faludy, Convocation Address, Roger Ebert, Film criticism, Liberal Arts, Published March 29, 2013. (Faludy was sent by Hungary's Communist government to its concentration camp in Recsk in 1949 for three years.)
23. Ibid.
24. Ibid.
25. Ibid.
26. Brother Christopher, *The Book that Changed My Life*, Ed. Coady and Johannessen, New York, Penguin Group, 2006, 47, 48.
27. Ibid.
28. First Kings 19:12.
29. Thomas Merton, *The Asian Journal of Thomas Merton*, New York, New Directions Publishing Corporation, 1975, 235.
30. Merton, *The Asian Journal*, vii.
31. St. John Climacus, *The Ladder of Divine Ascent*, New York, Paulist Press, 1982, 579-649 approx.
32. Ibid.
33. Ibid.
34. Climacus, 125.
35. Ibid.
36. Author unknown.
37. Ibid.
38. Thomas Merton, *Disputed Questions*, Farrar, Straus and Giroux, New York, June 1960, 100, 109.
39. Author unknown.
40. Scott Cairns, *Short Trip to the Edge: A Pilgrimage to Prayer*, Paraclete Press, February 2016, 203.
41. Ibid.
42. Ibid.
43. Ibid.
44. Thomas Merton, *Conjectures of a Guilty Bystander*, New York, Image Books, 1965, 158.
45. Ralph Waldo Emerson, *Emerson's Works*, Boston Houghton, Mifflin and Company, 1895, Vol 8, 33.
46. Jacob Needleman, *I am not I*, Berkeley, California, North Atlantic Books, 2006, xiii.
47. William Shakespeare, *Macbeth*, Act 5, scene 5, Independently Published, 2021.
48. Needleman, *I am not I*, Kindle, 181.
49. Ibid.
50. Ibid.

51. Ibid., 55.
52. Ibid.
53. Ibid.
54. Upjohn, Sheila. *All Shall Be Well: The Revelations of Divine Love of Julian of Norwich*. United Kingdom: Darton, Longman & Todd Limited, 2021.
55. Jerry Useem, "What was Volkswagen Thinking? On the origins of corporate evil—and idiocy." *The Atlantic*, Jan Feb. issue 2016.
56. Ibid.
57. Ibid.
58. Rainer Maria Rilke, *Rilke Book of Hours 3:1 The Book of Poverty and Death*, New York, Riverhead Books, The Penguin Group 1996, 191.
59. Rilke, *Rilke Book of Hours 3:1*, 191.
60. Rainer Maria Rilke, *Letters to a Young Poet*, New York W.W. Norton & Company, 1934, 35.
61. Ibid.
62. Ibid.
63. Ibid.
64. Dom Henri Le Saux, *A Christian Pilgrim in India, the Spiritual Journals of Swami Abhishiktananda*, Ed. Raimon Panikkar tr. David Fleming and James Stuart, Delhi, SPCK 1998, xv.
65. Malcolm Muggeridge, *A Third Testament*, Boston, Little, Brown and Company 1976, 86.
66. Thomas Merton was a Trappist monk. His autobiography is called *The Seven Storey Mountain*.
67. Malcolm Muggeridge, *Seeing Through the Eye: Malcolm Muggeridge on Faith*, San Francisco, Ignatius Press, 2005, xxi.
68. Ibid.
69. Malcolm Muggeridge, *A Twentieth Century Testimony*, Toronto Thomas Nelson Inc. 1978.
70. Malcolm Muggeridge, "The Great Liberal Death Wish." Posted on Orthodoxy Today (a retired website).
71. Ibid.
72. Ibid.
73. Ibid.
74. Ibid.
75. Ibid.
76. Alexander Solzhenitsyn, cited by Eric Metaxas, *Life, God, and Other Small Topics: Conversations from Socrates in the City*, New York, Penguin Books, 2012, 172.

77. Colin Wilson, *The Essential Colin Wilson,* London, Harrap, 1985, 103.
78. Bruce G. Charlton, "Everyday Consciousness is a liar—forty years of Colin Wilson," Bruce Charlton's Notions, charltonteaching.blogspot.com, August 2018.
79. *Finest Hour: The Battle of Britain EP 1 & 2*, Philip R Craig and Tim Clayton: https://youtu.be/uXu_PPca310.
80. Ibid.
81. Ibid.
82. T. S. Eliot, *The Complete Poems and Plays of T. S. Eliot,* United Kingdom: Faber & Faber, 2011, 363, 364.
83. Proverbs 1: 22b.
84. Evelyn Waugh, cited in Richard Gamble's *The Great Tradition: Classic Readings on What It Means to Be an Educated Human Being*, ISI Books, 2007, xvi.
85. Abhishiktananda, *The Further Shore,* quoted by Bettina Baumer in *Mysticism in Shaivism and Christianity,* New Delhi D.K. Print world, 1997, 37.
86. Louise A. A Vernon, *Heart Strangely Warmed*, United States: Herald Press, 2002.
87. C.S. Lewis, *Complete Works of C. S. Lewis (Illustrated)*, Delphi Classics, 2017. Ch ix.
88. Jovino de Guzman, *Tracing Nicholas of Cusa's Early Development*, Peeters Publishers Dec. 31, 2009, 222.
89. Ibid.
90. Acts 17:28.
91. St Augustine Confessions 3.6.11.
92. 2 Corinthians 5:17.
93. Jacob Needleman, *The Wisdom of Love—Toward a Shared Inner Life*, Sandpoint Id., Morning Light Press, Sandpoint ID 2005, 1 to 4.
94. William Butler Yeats, *When You Are Old: Early Poems, Plays, and Fairy Tales*. United States: Penguin Publishing Group, 2015, 151.
95. Needleman, *Wisdom*, 1 to 4.
96. Ibid.
97. John O'Donohue, *Anam Cara: A Book of Celtic Wisdom,* New York, Harpers Collins Books, 1997, 7.
98. Martin Lings, quoted by James. S. Cutsinger, a lecture delivered for the Narnia Clubs of New York Dec—C.S. Lewis as an Apologist and Mystic, Dec. 1998.
99. John O'Donohue, "The Voice of Your Own Soul," newstoryhub.com March 8, 2020.
100. John O'Donohue, *Anam Cara*, 7.

101 Gurumayi Chidvilasananda, *Kindle my Heart, Volume 2, Wisdom and Inspiration from a Living Master,* Prentice Hall Press, 1989, 15.
102 John 3:8.
103 Gurumayi, *Kindle,* 105,106.
104 Ibid.
105 Ibid.
106 Ibid.
107 Ibid.
108 Luke 17:21.
109 Ludwig Wittgenstein, *Philosophical Investigations,* cited by Judith Genova in *Wittgenstein, A Way of Seeing,* New York, Routledge, 1995, 201.
110 Metropolitan Anthony of Sourozh, website, Some Aspects of the Doctrine of Creation…
111 Rev 2:17.
112 Ibid.
113 Ibid.
114 Peter Kreeft, *The God Who Loves You,* Ann Arbor Michigan, Servant Books, 1988, 23.
115 George Appleton, referenced in Soul Nugget, A Daily Affirmation, a website, May 31, 2014.
116 David Pryce-Jones, "Treasons of the Heart," *The New Criterion*, Vol 40 No. 1, Sept. 2006.
117 Ibid.
118 David Pryce-Jones, "A Complete Moral Void," *The New Criterion*, March 2002.
119 Charles Moore, "A review of The Priest who thought Stalin was a Saint, by John Butter Scole," *the Telegraph,* Dec 25, 2011.
120 Ibid.
121 Ibid.
122 David Pryce-Jones, "Treasons of the Heart."
123 Kia Penso, Marvin Mudrick, *On Culture and Literature,* United States: Berkshire Publishing Group, 2017, 18.
124 Ibid.
125 Ibid.
126 Ibid.
127 Commonweal. United States: Commonweal Publishing Corporation, Volume 54, 1951, 188.
128 Ibid.
129 Ibid.
130 Ibid.

131. Ibid.
132. Daniel. N. Robinson, "Philosophy—Did the Greeks Invent It?" Lecture 2, The Great Ideas of Philosophy, 2nd Edition, Chantilly, Virginia, The Great Courses, 2004, 33.
133. Cushman, *Therapeia*, 289.
134. Ibid.
135. Wordsworth, William, "Ode: Intimations of Immortality from Recollections of Early Childhood," Germany: Hans eBooks, 2019.
136. Wordsworth, "Immortality."
137. Cushman, *Therapeia*, 60.
138. Huston Smith, *Forgotten Truth, The Common Visions of the World's Religions*, New York, HarperCollins 1976, 74.
139. C.S. Lewis, quoted by Jean Bethke Elshtain, Baggett, David, et al. *C.S. Lewis as Philosopher: Truth, Goodness and Beauty*, United States, Liberty University Press, 2017, 87.
140. Eric Metaxas, *Life, God, and Other Small Topics: Conversations from Socrates in the City*, United States: Plume Books, 2012, 142.
141. Raimon Panikkar, *Mysticism, Fullness of Life*, United States: Orbis Books, 2014, New York Orbis Books, Nook Book, 169.
142. Eric Donald Hirsch, Joseph F. Keto, James C. Trefil, *The New Dictionary of Cultural Literacy*, 204, 2002.
143. Stephen Harrod Buhner, "The Road Less Travelled," *Holistic Science Journal*, Vol. 2, Issue 4, Pathways, Earthlinks, UK.
144. Ibid.
145. Ibid.
146. Ibid.
147. Borghild Baldauf, Edited by Betinna Baumer & Karla Kumar, An "Icon of the Divine" Samvidullasah, Manifestation of Divine Consciousness, Swami Lakshman Joo Saint-Scholar of Kashmir Saivism—A Centenary Tribute, D.K. Print world Ltd. New Delhi, 204–212.
148. Ibid.
149. Ibid.
150. Ibid.
151. Ibid.
152. Raimon Panikkar, *Mysticism, Fullness of Life*, United States: Orbis Books, 2014, 169.
153. Peter L. Berger, *Questions of Faith, A Skeptical Affirmation of Christianity*, Malden, MA, Blackwell Publishing, 19
154. Ibid., 19.

[155] Ibid., 25.
[156] Ibid., 27.
[157] Ibid., 25.
[158] Ibid., 26.
[159] Ibid.
[160] Ibid., 27.
[161] Ibid.
[162] Ibid.
[163] Ibid., 29.
[164] Mathew 5:8.

CPSIA information can be obtained
at www.ICGtesting.com
Printed in the USA
LVHW080207100422
715792LV00010B/880